SIMON BRIGGS

Stiff Upper Lips and Baggy Green Caps

SIMON BRIGGS

Stiff Upper Lips and Baggy Green Caps

Quercus

First published in the UK in 2006 by Quercus
Updated edition published in 2007, 2009 by Quercus

This updated edition published in 2013 by
Quercus
21 Bloomsbury Square
London
WC1A 2NS

A CIP catalogue record for this book is available from the British Library

PB ISBN 978 1 78087 995 6
EBOOK ISBN 978 1 78087 398 5

Printed and bound in the UK by Clays Ltd, St Ives plc

10 9 8 7 6 5 4 3 2 1

FOR
BELLE

CONTENTS

DON'S DELIGHT: THE BRADMAN ERA: 1930–1948

IN SEARCH OF BRIGHTER CRICKET: 1950–1970

REIGN OF FIRE: 1970–1987

THE BAGGY GREEN MACHINE: 1989–PRESENT

FOREWORD BY GEOFF LAWSON

Although the term 'sledging' is an invention of the 1970s, the act goes back to the origins of the game itself. Out-talking your opponent is not solely the territory of cricketers – apparently Boris Spassky could whisper a sledge with the best of them. W.G. Grace could lay claim to being the finest sledger of the 19th century (as well as making a few runs and taking a few wickets).

Douglas Jardine had the arrogance of Grace plus the colonial background of the British Raj to drive his particular brand of on-field conversation. Jardine didn't much like Australians, but he had even less regard for those who were 'players' rather than 'gentlemen' – particularly if they were draught-horse bowlers.

Mike Brearley used language to manipulate the thoughts of his own players – particularly his bowlers – in the hope of improving their performance. Ian Chappell (perhaps the antipodean Jardine in dislike and design) had the firepower to back up his stinging rhetoric, and that always helps. Steve Waugh thought that 'mental disintegration' was a part of the game that deserved as much practice time as fielding. He simply re-coined the 'subtle as a sledgehammer' nomenclature and added a very hard, uncompromising edge to on-field exchanges that in past days may have brought more smiles (if only to the inner self of the antagonist) than grimaces.

England–Australia Test matches have maintained a position of predominance in the minds of spectators and the bodies of players since 1877. England versus Australia is *the* cricketing rivalry, the one that matters above all others: the Empire versus the Colony, Victorian manners versus Victorian Bushrangers, men representing the Queen against men representing the Queen's Land. Colourful language should be an ingredient of such rivalries – it beats taking your team off the field when the going gets tough. Bill Woodfull's only sledge during the 1932–33 Bodyline series was: 'There are two teams out there on the oval. One is playing cricket, the other is not.' Had he made the remark to Jardine rather than 'Plum' Warner, Jardine's reply would probably have been something in the vein of: 'Get stuffed!' And Merv Hughes and Fred Trueman would have approved. Economy of words is always helpful when sledging on the run – that is why bowlers will always have the edge over narcissistic batsmen.

Little has changed as the character of five-day cricket has maintained its predominance in the 21st century. The other unchangeable is the battle between bowlers and batsmen. Sure, the countries of England and Australia stand on either side of the conflict and words sometimes are exchanged, but batsmen have never understood bowlers. Mike Atherton became the captain of England in a time-honoured fashion – he played for Cambridge University and he was an opening bat. His description of my personal sledging was that 'it contained no overtones of humour or wit'. For those of us with science degrees who opened the bowling for their country, these words are of course a huge compliment. Athers's comment also presupposes that he could recognise either humour or wit – or both – when it was delivered in between 90mph cricket deliveries. A clear victory for sledgers, fast bowlers and optometrists the world over . . .

Coaches these days appoint 'designated sledgers', almost as a specialist role. If Mike Atherton thought intellect was fading in the late 1980s, then the current semantics are designed specifically with that trait in mind. Psychological advantage was almost a by-product, now it is the only ingredient, and that is not a desirable trend. Fortunately, history tells us that no matter what the advances in technology, training and preparation – the importance of a well-placed word will never be lost.

INTRODUCTION

England and Australia: two countries with a single language, a single head of state, and a single over-riding objective – to beat each other hollow at cricket. And all for what? A dingy little urn containing what one disenchanted player called 'a miserable handful of dust'.

The trophy is little more than a token, a six-inch symbol of sport's Hundred-and-Twenty Years' War. What makes the Ashes so perennially fascinating is the clash of competing civilisations. As Geoff Lawson says, it is 'The Empire versus the Colony, Victorian manners versus Victorian Bushrangers'. And as a fair dinkum Ocker himself – a country boy who learned to bowl on coir matting and anthill pitches – Lawson ought to know.

Cricket is a sport with a split personality. In England, many people still believe all that hoary old claptrap about it being a noble game. This soft-focus approach extends to the players: for most English amateurs, a game of cricket is an excuse for a little light exercise, a day away from the wife, and a few pints in the pub. Even at county level, Nasser Hussain has described the atmosphere as 'all very matey and lovey-dovey'.

The Australian strain is altogether more virile, more virulent. The concept of social cricket is quite alien to a people who can't go down to the beach without holding a tallest-sandcastle competition. From Adelaide to Wagga Wagga, Aussie cricket is full of what the locals call 'mongrel'. Wicketkeepers growl, close fielders yap, fast bowlers foam at the mouth. If the English game likes to see itself as a distinguished public school, Australia's is more of a borstal.

No team has ever won the urn by playing soft-ball. You only have to look at the great Ashes dynasties to understand that. First came Grace and Warwick Armstrong, serial lawbreakers both. Then Bradman, famously described as having 'a mind like a steel trap'. For England, the 1950s were a story of crime and punishment. Their crimes took the form of time-wasting

(Trevor Bailey) and pitch–doctoring (Jim Laker's 19–wicket haul). Their punishment consisted of five Tests against Australia's lethal 1958–59 chuckers. They must have felt like deserters facing an impromptu firing–squad.

The 1970s were the roughest decade of all. Ian Chappell and his mafia took Australian aggro to a new level. Their liberal use of verbals gave a new meaning to the term 'to sledge' – i.e. to put an opponent off his game by verbal means (for the derivation, see page 184). Sticks and stones may break your bones, but words – skilfully administered – can get you out.

Sledging was nothing new: even in the late 19th century, W.G. Grace and his brother E.M. were notorious for distracting the batsman by talking while the ball was being bowled. But Chappell's men upped the ante. They relentlessly piled on the pressure to see whether their opponents could take it or not.

There is a parallel here with what students of the art of seduction call a 'shit-test'. The genre's leading author Neil Strauss defines it as 'a question, demand, or seemingly hostile comment made by a woman intended to gauge whether a man is strong enough to be a worthy boyfriend or sexual partner'. Replace 'woman' with 'player' and 'boyfriend or sexual partner' with 'adversary', and there you have it.

If you pass the test, you have generally passed it for good. Paradoxically, sledging the best batsmen tends to be counter-productive. Graham Gooch and Allan Border are just two examples of players who lifted their games when the flak was flying. On a flat day, they would randomly pick on a close fielder and bark 'What the f*** are you looking at?' The backchat helped them focus on the task at hand.

But not everyone is so steady under fire. The textbook case of sledging in action came on Australia's 1993 tour of England, when Merv Hughes tore into England's ingénu Graeme Hick (see page 253). Australia exploited Hick's mental fragility just as

systematically as they would any other area of weakness –
whether a dodgy hook shot or a tendency to be yorked. Having
been written up as the new Bradman, Hick in fact turned out to
be the new Bo-Peep.

Sledging is often genuinely funny, offering a window into a
lifestyle sustained by dressing-room banter. It can be smart, sassy,
or sinister. But the joshing sometimes slips into mindless abuse,
and the game is better without it. In his autobiography, that arch-
sledger Steve Waugh writes: 'Direct abuse . . . should never be
allowed, while putting doubts in batsmen's minds by encouraging
each other and engaging in banter is all part of the game.
Occasionally abuse did arise, and it was an area we needed to clean
up as we were aware kids were copying our every move and such
an example was not the one we wanted to set.'

In recent years, the authorities have gradually stepped up their
campaign against sledging. In the 21st century, Hughes's merciless
Hick-baiting would almost certainly have earned him a ban.
Perhaps this is as it should be: if Hick had suffered all that bullying
and victimisation in any ordinary workplace, he could have sued
his tormentors into oblivion.

But the game's nannies are in danger of spoiling the fun.
Sledging and banter are part of cricket's rich heritage; no other
sport can offer such a treasure-trove of anecdotes and one-liners
(as this book demonstrates). Take the aggro out of cricket, and
you are left with nothing but rounders in whites.

Simon Briggs

ACKNOWLEDGEMENTS

Thanks are due to all the team at Quercus Books, especially my publisher Richard Milbank, who both provided the initial seed and then nurtured it carefully into life. I am also indebted to the many players who have answered my often asinine questions, especially my *Daily Telegraph* colleague Derek Pringle. Other consultees include Graham Gooch, Mike Gatting, Alec Stewart, Mike Atherton, Gladstone Small, Bob Woolmer and David Lloyd, while Geoff Lawson and Gideon Haigh have supplied Australasian expertise.

Of the many secondary sources I have used, Haigh has been by far the leading contributor. Apart from being the best cricket book I have read, Haigh's *The Summer Game* is also a mine of useful information. Apologies also to Simon Rae for pillaging his excellent works *W.G. Grace* and *It's Not Cricket*.

All the reading could not have been completed without the help of some exceptionally helpful librarians. Thanks especially to the ever-generous Peter Wynne-Thomas at Nottinghamshire, and to Adam Chadwick, Neil Robinson, Ken Daldry, and Glenys Williams at MCC. Two friends from the cricket press-box, Lawrence Booth and Richard Hobson, have also made their private libraries available.

Thanks finally to all my family. Jon and Julia have offered proof-reading skills and detailed input. And thanks, above all, to Leela and to Belle, who has (mostly) resisted the urge to sledge me for my absenteeism as a husband and father.

Simon Briggs
De Beauvoir Town
25 August 2006

THE BIRTH OF THE ASHES

1882–1911

PERFIDIOUS ALBION

Where does the story of the Ashes begin?
Some might point to the sarcastic obituary
notice in *The Sporting Times*, bemoaning the
death of English cricket. You could also make
a case for the Christmas party where Florence
Morphy presented England's captain with a
six-inch terracotta urn, a romantic keepsake
that would become a sporting icon.

The arguments will go on. But one thing we can say is that the
tone for the great Anglo-Australian rivalry was set at the very
beginning, by a dirty trick which backfired horribly on its
perpetrator. That man was W.G. Grace, a portly all-rounder
who shared a beard with Rasputin and a moral code with Al
Capone. His shamelessly unsporting gesture would set the tone
for the Ashes as we know them: 120-odd years of bouncers,
beamers, chuckers, sledgers, gamblers, bounders and cads.

The year was 1882, the place was The Oval, and the occasion
was the ninth Test match played between
England and Australia. England had won
their only previous match at home (in
1880), and when they had their upstart
cousins 110 for six in the second innings
– a meagre lead of 72 – another routine
victory seemed assured.

This was the moment when Sammy
Jones, the Australian No. 8 batsman, left
his crease to pat down a divot. Grace,

> **'Unless I'm crackers
> or something, I've
> scored a bloody sight
> more runs than that
> bearded old bugger.'**
> Geoffrey Boycott
> on W.G. Grace

1882: 1 TEST
AUSTRALIA 1–0

| E. PEATE (ENG.) | 8–71 |
| F.R. SPOFFORTH (AUS.) | 14–90 |

Fred 'The Demon' Spofforth raised hell in the Test that 'killed' English cricket. And from the corpse, rose the Ashes . . .

> **'W.G. Grace was by no conceivable standard a good man. He was a cheat on and off the cricket field.'**
>
> C.P. Snow, English novelist

behaving more like a pantomime villain than the most eminent Victorian of the age, whipped off the bails and appealed. The umpire was horrified, according to one account, but he whispered ruefully: 'If you claim it, sir, it is out.'

Grace might have thought his treachery expedient, but in fact it prompted one of the most dramatic fightbacks in cricket history. He had invoked the Demon, or, to give him his full name, Frederick 'The Demon' Spofforth. The first great Australian fast bowler, Spofforth stormed into the English dressing-room between innings to call Grace a cheat, and to warn him that 'This will lose you the match.' In his method, Spofforth sounds like a moustachioed Glenn McGrath: tall, spindly and metronomic. But there was a touch of England's Devon Malcolm in the way he roused himself to produce the spell of a lifetime. Just like Malcolm, who would famously tell the South Africans 'You guys are history,' after being hit on the helmet in 1994, Spofforth was an irresistible force as he ran through England with seven for 44. They were all out for 77,

Q: What do you get when you cross Glenn McGrath's method with Dennis Lillee's moustache? A: Frederick 'The Demon' Spofforth

just eight runs short of victory. Grace, top scorer with 32, was unimpressed. 'I left six men to get 30-odd runs and they could not get them,' he raged.

During his long reign as England captain, Mike Atherton used to complain that English newspapers were more interested in defeats than victories. On this occasion, his rule applied. '"The Decadence of English Cricket" was the theme of leader-writers in a hundred papers,' one periodical noted. A number of contemporary poets wrote verses about the match. (Years later it would furnish the subject-matter for the poem 'Eighty-five to Win' by no less a literary eminence than John Masefield, poet laureate from 1930 to 1967.) Stories circulated of one spectator who bit through his umbrella-handle in suspense, and another who suffered a fatal heart attack.

The most enduring comment came from an unlikely source. The Saturday after the game, Reginald Shirley Brooks published a mock obituary in *The Sporting Times*. The son of a distinguished editor of *Punch*, Brooks was a stereotypical boozy hack who chased actresses, gambled recklessly and drank himself to an early grave. Yet these 40 mocking words would earn him an immortality unmatched within the slobbish ranks of sportswriters.

In Affectionate Remembrance

OF

ENGLISH CRICKET,

WHICH DIED AT THE OVAL

ON

29th AUGUST, 1882,

Deeply lamented by a large circle of sorrowing friends and acquaintances.

R.I.P.

N.B.—The body will be cremated and the ashes taken to Australia.

W.G. GRACE – 'THE PERPETUAL SCHOOLBOY'

The father of the modern game, Grace was a curiously contradictory character. His biographer, Simon Rae, describes him as 'a classic case of arrested development, a perpetual schoolboy'. His team–mates often found him jolly and welcoming, a sort of Santa Claus in whites. But his approach to cricket was ferociously uncompromising. There were countless stories of cowed umpires, disputed tosses, and catches claimed on the half-volley. Grace's staggering first–class record – more than 54,000 runs and 2,800 wickets – gave the lie to the theory that cheats never prosper.

Though the word 'sledging' was not coined until the 1970s, our record of the phenomenon really starts with Grace. It is hard to imagine a more deflating put-down than his famous comment to an opposing bowler: 'They have come to watch me bat, not you bowl',

> **'They have come to watch me bat, not you bowl.'**
>
> W.G. Grace to an opposing bowler

especially when you consider its circumstances: Grace had just been bowled by the first ball of an exhibition match, but simply replaced the bails and carried on batting.

He was not above sledging his own team either. Captaining England in the Old Trafford Test of 1896, he conjured

The great W.G.: scorer of 54,211 first-class runs and capturer of 2,809 wickets. According to Viscount Cobham: 'He has one of the dirtiest necks I have kept wicket behind'

a fluky wicket by bringing wicketkeeper A.A. Lilley into the attack, then immediately sent him back behind the stumps with the cutting remark: 'You must have been bowling with your wrong arm.'

But the prize for the sledge of the 19th century goes to one of Grace's great rivals, Charles Kortright. The two men fought out a famous duel during Gloucestershire's first encounter with Essex in 1898. Kortright was that rare beast, an amateur fast bowler, but his sheer speed was probably greater than anything that Grace – now just past his 50th birthday – had ever faced.

The flashpoint came on the final day. Grace had already argued his way out of a blatant caught-and-bowled, and Gloucestershire needed only 52 more, when a furious Kortright summoned one of cricket's most venomous overs. The first ball struck Grace on the pad, right in front of all three. Not out, said the umpire. The second ball flicked the outside edge on its way through to the wicketkeeper. Not out, again. But the third smashed into the wicket, scattering the middle and leg stumps.

'Surely you're not going, Doc?' called Kortright, as Grace stomped off. 'There's still one stump standing.'

> **'Surely you're not going, Doc? There's still one stump standing.'**
> Fast bowler Charles Kortright clean bowls W.G.

WHEN IVO GOES BACK WITH THE URN

If W.G. Grace was the progenitor of sledging as we know it, the Hon. Ivo Bligh was the first England captain to talk in terms of winning or losing the Ashes. Arriving in Australia late in 1882, with the Oval defeat still fresh in the memory, Bligh told a dinner audience in Melbourne: 'We have come to beard the kangaroo in his den – and try to recover those Ashes.'

> **'We have come to beard the kangaroo in his den – and try to recover those Ashes.'**
> Hon. Ivo Bligh, 1882

Few of those present would have had any idea what Bligh was going on about. As a nation, 19th-century Australia was about as familiar with Brooks's obituary notice as it was with light opera. But there was one small group in the know. The England team had made the two-month crossing on the same steamship as Sir William Clarke, president of the Melbourne Cricket Club, and his entourage. Relations had become quite cordial, especially between Bligh and the Clarke family's music teacher, the beautiful but low-born Florence Morphy.

The Clarke family's estate, at Rupertswood in Victoria, would become a regular retreat for Ivo Bligh and his men. They were entertained royally, despite beating their hosts in the second and

A.G. STEEL (ENG.)   274 runs at 45.66 & 11 wkts at 17.72

G.E. PALMER (AUS.)   21 wkts at 18.90

Only three Tests had originally been scheduled, so England were agreed to have regained the Ashes when they went 2–1 up at Sydney. The fact that they then lost the extra match was conveniently ignored.

third Tests, and so becoming one of a select band of five English teams who have won back the Ashes in Australia.

During a Christmas party, Bligh received a keepsake from a group of ladies, including Morphy and Clarke's wife Janet. It was a red clay urn, just 10 cm in height, containing a handful of ashes (scholars still dispute whether these were the remnants of a bail, a ball or a veil). Inscribed on the side were the following six lines of doggerel:

When Ivo goes back with the urn, the urn;
Studds, Steel, Read and Tylecote return, return;
The welkin will ring loud,
The great crowd will feel proud,
Seeing Barlow and Bates with the urn, the urn;
And the rest coming home with the urn.

1884: 3 TESTS
ENGLAND 1–0

A.G. STEEL (ENG.)   212 runs at 53.00

W.L. MURDOCH (AUS.)   266 runs at 66.50

Steel had scored the first Ashes hundred in Sydney during the previous series. Now he added the second: his 148 at Lord's set up an innings victory.

1884–85: 5 TESTS
ENGLAND 3–2

W. BARNES (ENG.)   369 runs at 52.71 & 19 wkts at 15.36

F.R. SPOFFORTH (AUS.)   19 wkts at 16.10

Billy Barnes turned in brilliant all-round figures, but the decisive final Test hinged on Arthur Shrewsbury's 105. Shrewsbury was the subject of one of W.G. Grace's best-remembered quotes: when asked which player he would most like in his side, he replied 'Give me Arthur.'

Long before Monty Panesar, England had a brilliant slow left-armer in Johnny Briggs. A victim of epilepsy, he suffered a seizure during the Leeds Test of 1899, and died in Cheadle Asylum three years later

The verse may not have been up to Masefield's standards, but no matter: Morphy's courtship proved inspired. By the time Bligh left Australia, he had asked her to marry him, and the ceremony was conducted at Rupertswood a year later. They were married for 43 years, and when Bligh finally died in 1927, his widow – now Florence, Countess of Darnley – presented the tiny urn to the Marylebone Cricket Club, better known (in haughty defiance of the definite article) as MCC.

For the last 50 years, this smallest and most idiosyncratic of sporting trophies has been kept behind armoured glass in the Lord's museum. It is far too delicate to be waved around every other year by a bunch of half-cut sportsmen, so the urn we see being held up by the winning captain, or brandished in front of heaving crowds in Trafalgar Square, is in fact a replica – not much different from hundreds of others sold annually at the Lord's shop.

1886: 3 TESTS
ENGLAND 3–0

J. BRIGGS (ENG.) — 17 wkts at 17.76

F.R. SPOFFORTH (AUS.) — 16 wkts at 16.25

A second-rate Australian side were heavily beaten, especially in the final Test, where Grace's first Ashes century set up victory by an innings and 217. The leading bowler was Johnny Briggs, the slow left-armer whose Test career ended with an epileptic fit at Headingley in 1899.

1886–87: 2 TESTS
ENGLAND 2–0

G.A. LOHMANN (ENG.) — 16 wkts at 8.56

J.J. FERRIS (AUS.) — 18 wkts at 13.55

The highest score by either side was England's 184 at Sydney. Pitches were dreadful during this period, which partly explains how George Lohmann and J.J. Ferris finished up with the two lowest bowling averages in Test history.

1887–88: 1 TEST
ENGLAND 1–0

G.A. LOHMANN (ENG.)	**5–17 & 4–35**
R. PEEL (ENG.)	**5–18 & 4–40**

England dominated another low-scoring match thanks to Lohmann and Bobby Peel. A slow left-armer and fast drinker, Peel went on to take 101 Ashes wickets before he famously turned up drunk for a Yorkshire match in 1897 and was banned by Lord Hawke. Some witnesses even claimed that he peed on the pitch.

The 1888 Australian tourists: natty knitwear and some of the best pre-1970s facial hair. Fast bowlers Charlie 'The Terror' Turner and J.J. Ferris are respectively front row second left and back row far left

1888: 3 TESTS
ENGLAND 2–1

R. PEEL (ENG.) — 24 wkts at 7.54

C.T.B. TURNER (AUS.) — 21 wkts at 12.42

England came back strongly after losing the first Test on a turning track at Lord's. Peel was again their match-winner, the sharpest point of a lethal trident completed by Briggs and Lohmann. No batsman reached 100 runs in the series.

1890: 3 TESTS
ENGLAND 2–0

F. MARTIN (ENG.) — 12 wkts at 8.50

J.J. FERRIS (AUS.) — 13 wkts at 13.15

Frederick Martin came out of nowhere to take 12 for 102 in his first and only Ashes Test. Those figures would stand as the best on Ashes debut until Bob Massie's 16 for 137 at Lord's 82 years later.

THERE WAS AN OLD MAN WITH A BEARD

Ivo Bligh's rescue mission of 1882 was the start of a dominant period for England. They would monopolise the Ashes for eight consecutive series – a record which seemed unassailable until the modern Australians equalled it in 2002–03. Thank goodness for Andrew Flintoff, otherwise Ricky Ponting's mob would have made it nine.

England's reign ended with Grace's second tour of Australia. After demanding a tour fee of £3,000 (close to £150,000 in today's money), 'the Old Man' became a divisive and unpopular figure within his own team, let alone the opposition. The 1891–92 series was dogged by controversy. England lost at Melbourne, where they batted like hyperactive lemmings, then again at Sydney, where Grace refused to let the injured Harry Moses have a fielding substitute. Even a consolation win at Adelaide was soured by a row over the umpires, and by the time Grace left Australia, he stood accused of every crime save highway robbery.

'Grace is . . . a bad loser,' wrote Tom Horan, Australia's leading cricket reporter, 'and when he lost two of the Test matches in succession he lost his temper too, and kept on losing it right to the finish.' Grace's standing in the eyes of Australia was so low that many people were convinced by a spoof letter, originally published during his first visit in 1873–74, which was circulated again on his departure. This fabrication had Grace telling a friend that Australia 'is a fine country, but wants steeping for 24 hours in the sea to rid it of the human vermin crawling all over it'.

Such libels may explain why Grace was the target for another

Lord Sheffield's XI in Australia, 1891–92. Grace, the old goat, charged a tour fee equal to the rest of the players' salaries put together

famous fast-bowling salvo in 1896. Ernie Jones was Spofforth's successor, the second great speedster to come out of Australia. And like Harold Larwood after him, he was a coal-miner with a knack for hitting the seam.

The way Jones introduced himself to Grace has passed into legend. It was his first game in England, on a ropey wicket in Sussex, and one particularly fast delivery took off like a startled hare. When Grace threw his head back, the ball parted his beard, Moses-style. A pale-faced Grace burst out: 'Here, what is all this?' in his distinctive high-pitched voice. Jones's reply was memorably disingenuous: 'Sorry, Doctor, she slipped.' From this moment, Grace always referred to him as 'the fellow who bowled through my beard'.

Jones was one of those bowlers whose action became suspect when he searched for extra pace. His first ball of the Lord's Test was reported in the newspapers as 'a shie', and 'very difficult to distinguish from a throw'. Again, Grace was the recipient, and again he was caught off guard: the ball deflected off the top of his bat handle and flew over the wicketkeeper's head for four.

According to the journalist Home Gordon: 'The veteran looked volumes, [and] was so seriously discomfited that he took some time to recover his composure and then only after having made

'Sorry, Doctor, she slipped.'
Ernie Jones bounces W.G. Grace

some observations to the wicketkeeper, while the 12,000 spectators positively hummed, so general were their audible comments.'

From the fury of these exchanges, one cannot help wondering if Jones had read that fake letter. When they met at Lord's in 1899, Jones singed Grace's beard yet again – this time without bothering to make the ball bounce. His head-high full-toss constitutes the first recorded beamer in Test history.

Jones was something of a pioneer in the dark arts of fast bowling. During the 1897–98 Ashes series he had also become the first Test bowler to be no-balled for throwing. He was called both at Adelaide and Sydney, by an umpire – Jim Phillips – who considered himself the witchfinder-general of chuckers. But his embarrassment was nothing to that of England's batsmen, who fell to him 22 times during the course of the series. Needless to say, Australia regained the Ashes.

1891–92: 3 TESTS
AUSTRALIA 2–1

J.J. LYONS (AUS.) — 287 runs at 47.83

C.T.B. TURNER (AUS.) — 16 wkts at 21.12

Australia finally won back the Ashes after a lapse of nine years. England squandered a first-innings lead of 163 in the decisive second Test, collapsing to the medium-paced duo of Charlie 'The Terror' Turner and George Giffen. According to one contemporary account, 'The crowd howled and yelled, and cheered themselves hoarse.'

1893: 3 TESTS
ENGLAND 1–0

A. SHREWSBURY (ENG.) 284 runs at 71.00

J. BRIGGS (ENG.) 16 wkts at 18.31

A summer of fine weather produced an absolute run-glut, by the standards of the time. Shrewsbury was one of four England batsmen who averaged over 50.

1894–95: 5 TESTS
ENGLAND 3–2

T. RICHARDSON (ENG.) 32 wkts at 26.53

G. GIFFEN (AUS.) 475 runs at 52.88 & 34 wkts at 24.11

The series began in riveting fashion when England came from behind to win the Sydney Test by 10 runs (the only time, until Headingley 1981, a Test was won after following on). When Australia reached the fifth-day close on 113 for two, needing just 177, some England players assumed the worst, drinking late into the night. But when overnight rain turned the pitch into a 'sticky dog', England captain Andrew Stoddart stuck Bobby Peel in the shower to sober up. He proceeded to bag four of the final six wickets.

THE GOLDEN AGE
– OR WAS IT?

'You do well to love cricket, for it is more free
from anything sordid, anything dishonourable,
than any game in the world.' So said Lord Harris,
a snobbish aristocrat who captained England,
governed Bombay, and generally did his best
to get through life with his pads on.

As we have already seen, Harris was quite wrong. But if he was ever
right, it must have been during cricket's 'Golden Age'. This halcyon
era is generally agreed to have stretched from the turn of the century
to the First World War – or, to put it another way, from Grace's last
Test (1899) to the appointment of Warwick Armstrong, an equally
large and uncompromising figure, as Australian captain in 1920.

During the Golden Age, fair play was the only kind of play.
Bowlers pitched the ball up, batsmen placed artistry above dogged
accumulation, and the lion lay down with the lamb. It was an era
not only of spotless sportsmanship but of teeming talent. England's
team for the 1902 Edgbaston Test is widely considered the strongest
in history, featuring Wilfred Rhodes (who had a Test batting
average of 30.19) at No. 11.

If there was one man who captured the debonair spirit of
the age, it was the ultimate dasher – Australia's Victor Trumper.
While Trumper's statistics – 3,163 runs at 39.04 – might not seem
exceptional, his worth can be measured in the admiration of his
peers. A.C. MacLaren, not a man lacking in self-esteem, once said
with a snort: 'My best innings compared with one by Victor was
shoddy – hack work!'

Len Hutton told a story that summed up Trumper's approach
to cricket – and life. During a tour match at Headingley, he refused

Victor Trumper, the acme of elegance. According to one contemporary, he even folded his shirt-sleeves in a 'trim and artistic' sort of way

to play any attacking strokes at a young collier making his Yorkshire debut. His thinking was revealed afterwards, when he admitted that he hadn't wanted to 'spoil that lad's chance of getting a living in an easier way than heaving coal'.

Lord Harris admired Trumper's style, if not his egalitarian instincts. But he had rather less time for Kumar Shri Ranjitsinhji, the self-styled 'Prince of Nawanagar', who was emerging as England's finest player. As a selector for the Lord's Test of 1896, Harris refused to countenance the idea of 'Ranji' – born in Sarodar in India but educated at Cambridge – playing Test cricket for his adopted country. Harris valued fairness in all things, especially skin.

Fortunately, as far as cricket's diversity is concerned, Harris's blackballing wasn't sustainable. Ranji was awarded his Test debut in the very next match at Old Trafford, and proved the point with innings of 62 and 154 not out. The *Manchester Guardian* enthused: 'Our Indian ally showed us how the Australian bowling should be met. Grace has nothing to teach him as a batsman.'

Ranji was a mould-breaker both on and off the field. He defied the conventional wisdom that there was a 'correct' stroke to play to any given ball, preferring to invent his own variations. His signature shot was the leg-glance: just like Mohammad

'Our dark Blue.'
A reference to Ranjitsinhji
in *The Cambridge Review*

Azharuddin, 80-odd years later, he liked to step across his stumps and whip the ball through square-leg.

The leg-glance may be part of the furniture now, but in the 1890s it was revolutionary, even transgressive. It met with suspicion around the counties, as we can see from the famous quote, ascribed to Yorkshire's Ted Wainwright, that Ranji 'never played a Christian stroke in his life'. To plain, God-fearing Englishmen, it was as if all the mystery of the Orient had been distilled into a single flick of the wrists.

Ranji's contempt for orthodoxy would be taken a stage further by his nephew Kumar Shri Duleepsinhji. Playing for the Hindus against the Parsis in 1928, Duleepsinhji produced the first recorded instance of the reverse-sweep, which met with an (unsuccessful) appeal for unfair play. But even the leg-glance was too much for Lord Harris to take. When England suffered eight consecutive Test defeats in the early 1920s, Harris blamed Ranji and his conjuror's tricks for corrupting a generation of batsmen.

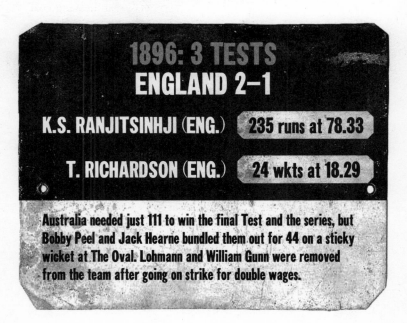

1896: 3 TESTS
ENGLAND 2–1

K.S. RANJITSINHJI (ENG.) — 235 runs at 78.33

T. RICHARDSON (ENG.) — 24 wkts at 18.29

Australia needed just 111 to win the final Test and the series, but Bobby Peel and Jack Hearne bundled them out for 44 on a sticky wicket at The Oval. Lohmann and William Gunn were removed from the team after going on strike for double wages.

'Yes, he can play, but he must have a lot of Satan in him.'

Anon. spectator on Ranji, as reported by C.B. Fry

Prince Kumar Shri Ranjitsinhji: 'He is not a miser hoarding up runs,' wrote A.G. Gardiner, 'but a millionaire spending them'

1897–98: 5 TESTS
AUSTRALIA 4–1

J. DARLING (AUS.) 537 runs at 67.12

E. JONES (AUS.) 22 wkts at 25.13

Joe Darling became the first man to pass 500 runs in an Ashes rubber, but the series is best remembered for Clem Hill's 188 at Melbourne. England's plans relied on fast bowler Tom Richardson, 'the swarthy giant', but his spreading waistline may have contributed to a bowling average of 35.

CHARLES III AND THE MAHARAJAH

Even the greatest novelist would struggle to invent a pair of characters as outlandish as Ranjitsinhji and his long-standing friend and ally C.B. Fry. Ranji's story could have come straight from the pages of Kipling. He claimed to be a prince, on the rather flimsy basis that a Maharajah had once considered adopting him. But the myth would eventually become reality. When Ranji returned to India in 1907, it was as the Maharajah Jam Saheb of Nawanagar.

> **'In form and feature he might have stepped out of an Athenian frieze.'**
>
> Harry Altham on C.B. Fry

Fry's curriculum vitae was even more improbable. His biographer Iain Wilton writes that by the age of 21 he had 'scored a first-class hundred, secured two successive triple Blues, won an England cap at football and equalled a world athletics record'. The polymath's polymath, Fry would inspire a comic-book strip – Wilson of *The Wizard* – that spent 40 years charting its hero's sporting triumphs.

Fry was the dominant figure in his time at university, and collected a range of admiring nicknames, including Lord Oxford, Almighty and Charles III. His Oxford college, Wadham, contained two future cabinet ministers, yet it was wittily described as 'Fry and small fry'. But when he joined Ranji at Sussex, and took his first turn around the county circuit, he was known simply as 'Cocky'.

Perhaps it was that very hauteur that caught the eye of

W.G. Grace. At Trent Bridge in 1899, England's opening pair boasted the four most famous initials in the game. As they walked down the pavilion steps, the corpulent W.G. wagged a finger at the spry young C.B. – 'Look here, Charlie Fry, remember I am not a sprinter like you.' Fry was eventually bowled for 50 in his first Ashes innings, though he later lamented that: 'We lost innumerable singles on the off-side, and I never dared to call W.G. for a second run to the long-field.'

Though Fry's Ashes career stretched for 13 years, he would never tour Australia. His reluctance had less to do with Aussie bouncers than the consequences of vacating the crease back home: given a prolonged absence, there was every possibility that his wife Beatrice might have rekindled her affair with Charles Hoare. (By the time of their marriage, she had already had two illegitimate children by Hoare, and even her third was said to resemble her lover more than her husband.)

'Look here, Charlie Fry, remember I am not a sprinter like you.'
W.G. Grace, 1899

Fry's marital problems would strike a chord with many a modern player. Unfortunately, they also delayed his promotion to the England captaincy until 1912, the year of the Triangular Tournament. This one-off experiment was arranged for the benefit of South Africa, the gooseberry in the great Ashes romance. But a summer of terrible weather, plus South Africa's determined impersonation of modern-day Bangladesh, meant that the whole shooting-match came down to the very last game: England v Australia at The Oval.

Presented with a wet pitch, Fry refused to start England's innings until mid-afternoon on the first day – a successful tactic, but an unpopular one with the crowd, who barracked him when he went out to bat. Once victory had been sealed, and the fickle fans won over, he refused to go out on the balcony to acknowledge the cheers. Ranji encouraged him with the words: 'Charles, be your noble self', but Fry replied sulkily: 'The time for them to cheer was when I went in to bat to save England, and not now we've won the match.' It was to be his last Test.

Charles Burgess Fry: scholar-batsman supreme, FA Cup finalist for Southampton, world-record holder for the long jump – and to date the only England batsman to be offered the throne of Albania

In the late 1920s, Charles III very nearly became a king for real. Ranji had been appointed as one of India's three delegates to the League of Nations, and took his old friend along as an assistant. Fry's autobiography, *Life Worth Living*, tells the story: 'So it was that one day when I went to see him at breakfast in bed, Ranji enquired casually: "Carlos, would you like to be King of Albania?" I accepted on the nail. I was willing to be king of any willing nation. "Well," he said, "the bishop is coming to see me about it tomorrow."'

From the various negotiations that Albania had with Lord Headley, we can be confident that this offer was not an idle one. Their job spec required an Englishman with an independent means of £10,000 per annum. Sadly, Fry's means could not quite run to that, and Ranji soon abandoned the idea of sponsoring him. He remained a commoner, if a uniquely distinguished one.

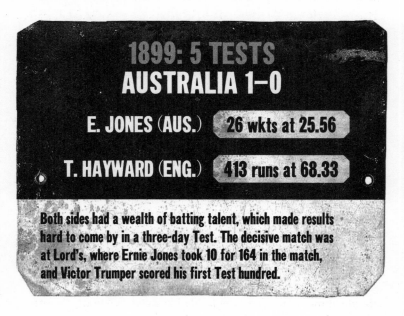

1899: 5 TESTS
AUSTRALIA 1–0

E. JONES (AUS.) 26 wkts at 25.56

T. HAYWARD (ENG.) 413 runs at 68.33

Both sides had a wealth of batting talent, which made results hard to come by in a three-day Test. The decisive match was at Lord's, where Ernie Jones took 10 for 164 in the match, and Victor Trumper scored his first Test hundred.

SYDNEY BARNES: CLASS WARRIOR

As far as Debrett's was concerned, Ranji and Fry were never more than pretenders to the throne. But they were emperors compared to most of the men who bowled to them. With a few exceptions, batsmen were already established as the gentry of the game. Bowlers were the weary labourers. In the words of Wilfred Rhodes, 'We don't play this game for fun.' The 'players' – or professionals – rarely kicked up a fuss over their second-class status. They needed the money too badly. But there was one man who refused to bow the knee to anyone. Sydney Barnes was both the finest bowler of his day and the most insubordinate fellow that any amateur had the misfortune to encounter. He won his captain matches while driving him round the twist.

A.C. MacLaren was the first England captain to strike a deal with this devil. It was MacLaren who picked the 28-year-old Barnes for the 1901–02 tour of Australia, even though he was little more than a Lancashire League bowler at the time. After an exploratory net session at Old Trafford, MacLaren recalled: 'He thumped me on the right thigh. He hit my gloves from a length. He actually said: "Sorry, Sir!" and I said "Don't be sorry Barnes, you're coming to Australia with me."'

It is a nice story, but a hard one to credit. Barnes never apologised to anyone, let alone a batsman and supposed social

'Put on to bowl at the "wrong" end, he would scowl and sulk and develop mysterious physical disorders, sprains and strains.'

Bernard Hollowood on S.F. Barnes

superior. His attitude was captured by his Lancashire League team-mate Bernard Hollowood, a future editor of *Punch*, who wrote: 'He was forever kicking against the pricks and quarrelling with the establishment.' Nowadays, Barnes would be a republican. Then, he was just a royal pain in the arse. MacLaren had plenty of time to rue his error on the two-month steamship journey to Australia. As the *Omrah* wallowed in heavy seas in the Bay of Biscay, he uttered the classic line: 'At least if we go down we'll take that bugger Barnes down with us.'

Once the ship had docked, Barnes turned his baleful stare on the Australians. It is doubtful whether any bowler has so mastered the mechanics of his craft. Barnes could do anything – pace, swing or spin – and he put so much work on the ball that it tore chunks out of the pitch. Here is Clem Hill's description of the one that

According to Neville Cardus, Sydney Barnes held a cricket ball 'sensitively, like a violinist a fiddle'. He also possessed a temper that frightened the life out of his own team-mates, let alone his opponents

got him at Melbourne: 'The ball pitched outside my leg stump, safe to push off my pads, I thought. Before I could "pick up" my bat, my off stump was knocked silly.' Just over a century later, England's Mike Gatting would be castled in similar fashion by another Ashes newcomer – a brash, blond leg-spinner named Shane Warne.

Barnes was a whole attack rolled into one, which may explain why so many captains insisted that he bowl all day. On MacLaren's tour, however, the tactic backfired. Pounding his way through a punishing 133 overs in the first two Tests, Barnes acquired 19 Test victims and a dicky knee. England did eventually go down, by a whopping 4–1 margin, but only because 'that bugger Barnes' was not there to bowl the Aussies out.

Though we have no specific accounts of Barnes sledging the opposition, he was clearly an intimidating presence. His *Wisden* obituary said 'There was a Mephistophelian aspect about him', a point developed in Hollowood's personal account: 'I was afraid of Barnes, afraid of his scowling displeasure, his ferocious glare, his crippling silences and his humiliating verbal scorn, and I played with and against him only when he was beginning to mellow.' Over three tours of Australia, he took on an ogrish quality, to the point where mothers only had to mention his

'At least if we go down we'll take that bugger Barnes down with us.'

England captain
A.C. MacLaren

> **'There's only one captain of a side when I'm bowling. Me.'**
> S.F. Barnes

name to frighten their children.

In fact, Barnes's own captains usually came in for a harder time than the opposition. 'There's only one captain of a side when I'm bowling,' he once insisted. 'Me.' In the first Test of England's 1911–12 tour, J.W.H.T. Douglas dared to risk the ogre's wrath by opening England's attack with the amateur left-armer Frank Foster and his own medium-paced seamers. 'That's all very well, Mr Douglas,' came the withering reply, 'but what am I 'ere for?' The great man sulked through the rest of the match.

THE FIRST GREAT SERIES

The 1902 Ashes series brought together many of the characters we have already met. Australia's batting and bowling were led by Trumper and Jones respectively; England fielded Ranji, Fry and Barnes under the captaincy of MacLaren. It was Test cricket's first great series, climaxing in two cliffhanging finishes that have passed into legend.

How odd, then – and yet how typical of cricket – that the man who did most to decide the outcome appeared on neither team. That man was Lord Hawke, the grandee who ran Yorkshire cricket and an England selector for ten years. Hawke was a useful batsman himself, good enough to score 13 first-class hundreds. But when it came to picking teams, he might as well have used a ouija board.

The series started sensibly enough. Australia would have been well beaten at Edgbaston, where Rhodes skittled them for 36, if rain had not intervened (as it did at Lord's, reducing the second Test to a mere 38 overs). England then went 1–0 down in the only Test match ever played at Sheffield's Bramall Lane. The recalled Barnes took six for 49, swinging the ball through the heavy, smoggy air generated by dozens of steel furnaces. But Australia, bolstered by Clem Hill's 119, stood firm. Bad light and pollution were blamed for the result, proving that the English always did have a flair for excuses.

Worse was to come in the fourth Test at Old Trafford, the venue for one of the most catastrophic selectorial cock-ups in history. Historians are still groping towards an explanation for

Lord Hawke, the biggest wig in Yorkshire cricket and England's selectorial saboteur. During his 10-year reign, players went in and out of fashion faster than the latest hats

this schemozzle. Was sheer incompetence to blame? Or did it all stem from bad blood between Hawke and MacLaren? After all, the Yorkshireman and the Lancastrian had been fighting their own private Wars of the Roses for years.

Whatever the answer, the upshot was an England team missing four of its strongest players. The axe had fallen on Barnes, on Fry, on George Hirst, and on Gilbert 'The Croucher' Jessop, a fiery Gloucestershire all-rounder who hit the ball like a jackhammer. When MacLaren saw the squad, he must have wondered whether Lord Hawke and his selectors were batting for the right side. 'My God!' he cried out. 'Look what they've given me! Do they think we are playing the blind asylum?'

So it was that England's last bowling spot went to Fred Tate, an unheralded medium-pacer from Sussex. His single Test appearance was such a disaster that he is commonly referred to as 'Poor' Fred Tate. In the second innings of a low-scoring match, he found himself fielding in an unfamiliar position at deep square-leg when Joe Darling lofted an easy catch. It was the key moment of the match. Tate, needless to say, dropped it.

England were set 124 to win, and when MacLaren was third out, he feared the worst. 'I've thrown away the match and the bloody rubber!' he groaned, flinging his bat down on the nearest locker. It was a typically selfish reaction, but MacLaren's team-mates were not done yet; indeed, they had carried the score to 117 by the time the ninth wicket fell.

Enter England's No. 11, the ill-fated Tate. Fame beckoned when his first ball glanced off the inside-edge to the fine-leg boundary. But the fourth rattled his stumps. Tate was devastated: one account describes him calling a hansom cab, drawing the blinds and weeping. Eventually, he composed himself enough to tell a team-mate: 'Never mind, I've got a little kid at home who will make it up for me.' Maurice Tate, then seven years old, would go on to take 155 Test wickets.

The 1902 rubber was indeed lost, but the fifth Test at The Oval was another cracker. Again, England had to bat last on a wet pitch, and again they seemed to be sinking fast at 48 for five – still 215 short of victory. That was the moment when Jessop, restored to the side, struck a wild-eyed 104 in just 77 minutes – still the

1902: 5 TESTS
AUSTRALIA 2–1

H. TRUMBLE (AUS.) | 26 wkts at 14.26

HON. F.S. JACKSON (ENG.) | 308 runs at 44.42

'It was in the Selection Room that the Rubber was lost,' wrote Gilbert Jessop. Australia snatched a memorable three-run win to seal the series at Old Trafford, where Fred Tate was (unfairly) cast as England's villain. But a lightning-fast Jessop hundred at The Oval, followed by *that* last-wicket stand between George Hirst and Wilfred Rhodes, made sure the home side finished on an upbeat note.

Gilbert Jessop was known as 'The Croucher' for his distinctive stance. As a contemporary versifier put it, he 'wrecked the roofs of distant towns / when set in an assault'

> ## 'My God! Look what they've given me! Do they think we are playing the blind asylum?'
> ### A.C. MacLaren reacts
> ### to his England XI

fastest century in Ashes history. Fry would later claim that 'No man has ever driven the ball so hard, so high and so often in so many different directions.'

It was an innings of extraordinary chutzpah at a time of crisis. Yet even Jessop's blitz was not enough to blow Australia away. When he flicked a catch to short-leg, England's tailenders had a chance to redeem themselves. They kept worrying away at the total until the equation had been reduced to its simplest form: 15 runs to get, one wicket in hand. The last pair was that grittiest of Yorkshire double acts, George Hirst and Wilfred Rhodes. Legend has it that when Rhodes came out, Hirst went over to him and said 'We'll get 'em in singles, Wilfred.' But this tale is just that: a tale. As Rhodes put it later, 'I don't think any cricketer would believe it. There'd have been just as much sense if he'd said: "We'll get 'em in sixes."'

As the target drew closer, the tension recalled that of the original Ashes Test of 1882. According to a contemporary report: 'Some laughed, some could not sit still, others dug their nails into their hands, while one old man was seen folding up his gloves quite methodically and making a parcel of them in his scorecard – quite beside himself.' This time, though, England were not to be denied. With the scores level, Rhodes pushed the ball firmly past mid-on and ran all the way into the onrushing crowd. The ensuing pandemonium even reached the press-box, where Charles Stewart Caine, the editor of *Wisden*, is reported to have gone wild with excitement, standing up in his seat and waving his hat.

FROM BOSANQUET TO GREGORY:
CRICKET'S ARMS RACE
1903–1929

THE GOOGLY: CRICKET'S WRONG 'UN

Anglo–Australian Test matches were fast becoming the definitive sporting events of the day. Yet the concept of the Ashes had largely been forgotten. That changed after 1903–04, when Pelham ('Plum') Warner led an indifferent-looking team to victory in Australia. Warner, an Establishment man if ever there was one, liked the idea of painting himself as a modern-day Ivo Bligh, and he would celebrate England's triumph in a bestseller entitled *How We Recovered The Ashes*.

> **'A term often applied to felons, divorcées and homosexuals.'**
> Cricket historian David Frith on 'the wrong 'un'

'Plum' Warner had an unlikely secret weapon in Bernard Bosanquet, his Oxford University and Middlesex team-mate. Most captains would have raised their eyebrows at Bosanquet's experimental new delivery, the googly, and picked a steady medium-pacer instead. But Warner chose to ignore the fact that Bosanquet's googlies regularly bounced four times on their way to the batsman. He was fresh, he was different, and – best of all – he was an amateur.

Bosanquet's art was based on deception. The googly looked like a leg-break but turned in the opposite direction. Attempts to crack the code were further hampered by Bosanquet's own vagueness about what he was bowling and where it might land. One Australian newspaper commented: 'He is the worst length bowler in England and yet he is the only bowler the Australians fear.'

When he bowled in tandem with England's other spinner, Wilfred Rhodes, it was a case of Bosanquet from one end, tourniquet from the other. In the first Test, Rhodes's niggardly second-innings figures of 40.2–10–94–5 prompted Trumper to exclaim: 'For God's sake, Wilfred, give me a minute's rest.'

B.J.T. Bosanquet, inventor of the googly. Bosanquet devised his secret weapon while playing 'Twisti-Twosti', a game whose object was to bounce a tennis ball across a table so that it eluded the player opposite

'Poor old googly! It has been subjected to ridicule, abuse, contempt, incredulity – and survived them all.'

B.J.T. Bosanquet, inventor of the googly, 1924

Bosanquet, by contrast, managed just seven maidens in the whole series. He was the big, clumsy labrador to Rhodes's Yorkshire terrier. But he repaid Warner's faith during the decisive fourth Test at Sydney. In one of those bewitching spells that wrist-spinners are prone to conjure up from nowhere, he captured six second-innings wickets in less than an hour's play.

'Except when Rhodes and Arnold put Victoria out for 15, nothing more startling was done with the ball during the tour,' wrote a jubilant Warner in *How We Recovered The Ashes*. 'Unkind people said ere this that I "ran" Bosanquet into this team because he was a friend of mine . . . [but] when he gets a length he is, on hard wickets, about the most difficult bowler there is.'

Like every other cricketing innovation, the googly met with suspicion and scepticism. As usual, most pundits sympathised with the batsman, arguing that the game had been a finer thing when a fellow could stand tall and drive through the off-side with impunity. But the MCC fought shy of banning it, presumably because it kept winning Tests for England.

The South Africans were quick to pick up the googly habit. On their 1907 tour, they sent as many as four mystery spinners to England. But it was not until the advent of 'Ranji' Hordern, who played almost a decade after Bosanquet's breakthrough, that the Aussies cottoned on. In Australia the googly was known as 'the wrong 'un', a term which – as the cricket historian David Frith has pointed out – was 'often applied to felons, divorcées and homosexuals'.

SLINGS AND ARROWS

Warner's account of the 1903–04 tour maintains an Olympian sort of tone. His writing is from the same school of understated Englishness as a *Pathe News* broadcast. But there was one subject that could turn Warner into a proto-Richard Littlejohn – and that was the behaviour of Australian crowds.

Sydney was always the feistiest venue. England played two Tests there under Warner, and the first featured a near riot over a run-out decision given against Clem Hill by umpire Bob Crockett. A chorus of boos and hisses prompted Warner and his opposite number Monty Noble to sit down on the pitch for a few minutes. When they attempted to restart, the fans jeered: 'How much did you pay Crockett, Warner?', 'Have you got your coffin ready, Crockett?' and 'Which gate are you leaving by, Crockett?'

Crockett, a Melburnian, was again in the firing-line when the teams returned to Sydney. This time, the crowd grew incensed by the umpires' decision to stay off the field for 80 minutes on the second day. There was a light drizzle in the air, to which the spectators added a hail of bottles. Soon the cycle-track around the outfield was covered in broken glass.

This unhappy spectacle spurred Warner into the following flight of fancy: 'I can imagine an official rushing to the telephone and ringing up the War Minister. Across the wire comes: "Send troops." "What for?" "International match now on. Crowd on hill armed to the teeth with umbrellas, bottles, melon skins and rude language, advancing determinedly on wicket. Three

R.E. ('Tip') Foster, the only man to captain England at both cricket and football, got England off to a winning start with 287 at Sydney – still the highest score by a Test debutant, or a tourist in Australia. This was the first team to be organised by MCC, who took over when MacLaren tried to postpone his planned tour until 1904–05, then controversially left him out of the party.

policemen and groundsman's dog doing good work. Umpires Crockett and Argall retreating to the mountains."

'This is what might have been. This is what it will certainly come to: "A cable has been received stating that the English Cricket Team has left London for Australia accompanied by complete Army Corps. General French is in command, and the opinion is freely expressed that this time, at any rate, the cricketers will be adequately protected. Several batteries of the new Maxim gun go out with the troops, and they are expected very effectually to sweep the hill on the Sydney ground whence in the past so many onslaughts on the players and umpires have issued."'

There is a delicious irony in Warner's later return to Australia as manager of Douglas Jardine's Bodyline tour. Mounted police were indeed required during the Adelaide Test of 1932–33, but only because England's fast bowlers were doing their best to turn cricket into a blood sport.

Every touring team suffered the slings and arrows of outrageous crowds. Ranjitsinhji was badly barracked in 1897–98, prompting his Australian opponent Frank Iredale to write apologetically: 'The people here view all people not actually white as alien.' Barnes was also booed during his masterful spell of 11–7–6–5 at Melbourne in 1911–12; his typically uncompromising response was to throw down the ball and fold his arms until it stopped. Even Andrew Stoddart, one of the most popular England captains to tour Australia, made public reference to 'the insults which have been poured upon me and my team during our journey through this country'.

English players may have felt these barbs more sharply because their own crowds were so small and meek. Back home, cricket-watching was a pastime for gentlemen, and play was regularly suspended just because an aeroplane was passing overhead. So when England teams looked at the thousands of

1905: 5 TESTS
ENGLAND 2–0

HON. F.S. JACKSON (ENG.) — 492 runs at 70.28 & 13 wkts at 15.46

W.W. ARMSTRONG (AUS.) — 252 runs at 31.50 & 16 wkts at 33.62

By the end of his famous summer, Jackson stood atop both the batting and bowling averages. He won all five tosses as well. Trumper's highest score in the series was just 31.

farmers and furriers who filled the Sydney Cricket Ground, they must have felt like Christians entering the Colosseum. By the time they returned home, most English tourists took the same view of Australian crowds that Bertie Wooster did of his aunts. 'At the core they are all alike. Sooner or later, out pops the cloven hoof.'

1907–08: 5 TESTS
AUSTRALIA 4–1

W.W. ARMSTRONG (AUS.)   410 runs at 45.55 & 14 wkts at 25.78

G. GUNN (ENG.)   462 runs at 51.33

England only managed one win but at least it was an exciting one. A 39-run stand between Sydney Barnes and Arthur Fielder clinched the second Test by a single wicket. Several players turned down the terms offered by MCC, making way for Jack Hobbs's debut.

WARWICK ARMSTRONG: NEW GRACE OR DISGRACE?

In the stands, and on the field, a new and discordant note was beginning to disrupt the elegant harmonies of the Golden Age. It found its most obvious embodiment in Warwick Armstrong, an ultra-competitive Australian all-rounder who treated cricket as war. Even against sub-standard opposition, Armstrong did not know how to throttle back; he would happily have scored 300 against his son's school team.

Armstrong's biographer, Gideon Haigh, paints him as the first modern cricketer. He certainly took a reductive view of the game. When he batted, his aim was to eliminate risk; when he bowled, he tried to slow the scoring rate by sending his gentle top-spinners down the leg-side. As one contemporary cricket writer put it: 'I would sooner see five minutes of Trumper than two hours of Armstrong.'

It was Armstrong's very disregard for the niceties that made him dangerous. But just *how* dangerous would only become clear after the Great War. Appointed captain for the 1920–21 series, he inflicted a 5–0 whitewash on J.W.H.T. Douglas's Englishmen. There

'Warwick Armstrong is portentous,' wrote an English journalist in 1921. 'He reminds one as he approaches of a character out of Conrad; there is an air of suppressed force about him'

have been many feared captains of Australia: Bradman, Chappell, Border and Waugh, to name just a few. But Armstrong, and more recently Ricky Ponting, remain the only ones who have made a clean sweep of the Ashes.

Armstrong was an intimidating presence, 6ft 3in tall and built like a WWF wrestler. Towards the end of his career, when his weight touched 22 stone, he must have made Merv Hughes look like a supermodel. And he was also a proficient sledger, quite capable of matching Hughes profanity for profanity. Obscene comments could hardly have been reported in the fastidious newspapers of the time, even if there had been stump microphones to pick them up. But no one can doubt

> ## 'The chief offender was Warwick Armstrong, who got very nasty and unsportsmanlike, refusing to accept the umpire's decision.'
> Jack Hobbs, 1909

that Armstrong gave Jack Hobbs a right mouthful during the Headingley Test of 1909.

'The Australians made a rare fuss,' wrote Hobbs, who had just survived an appeal for hit wicket. 'They gathered together in the field and confabulated. The chief offender was Warwick Armstrong, who got very nasty and unsportsmanlike, refusing to accept the umpire's decision. This upset me. I did not know whether I was standing on my head or my heels, with the consequence that two balls later I let one go, never even

1909: 5 TESTS
AUSTRALIA 2–1

W.W. ARMSTRONG (AUS.) 189 runs at 23.62 & 14 wkts at 20.92

W. BARDSLEY (AUS.) 396 runs at 39.60

England used 25 players in a summer of selection blunders. After winning the first Test, they went to Lord's without a single recognised fast bowler. At The Oval, Warren Bardsley became the first man to score a century in each innings of a Test.

attempting to play it, and it bowled me. I still bear this incident in mind against Armstrong.'

The similarities with W.G. Grace are hard to ignore. Armstrong and 'the Doctor' were the two great book-ends of early Ashes cricket. Grand in manner, imposing in physique, they dominated the lesser men around them, just as one suspects they would have dominated any field or era. And there was one other thing they had in common. Neither could see a belt without hitting below it.

Armstrong's finest piece of gamesmanship outdid even Grace for sheer cheek. It came at The Oval, two games after the Hobbs bust-up, as England pressed for the win that would square the series. At the fall of the fourth wicket, the young Kent all-rounder Frank Woolley walked out expecting to face his first ball in Test cricket. But Armstrong kept him waiting fully 19 minutes while he bowled a series of looseners. According to the sportswriter E.H.D. Sewell: 'This unofficial interval was brought about almost entirely by Armstrong bowling several trial balls from the pavilion end, somewhat sketchy attempts being made to stop them at the other . . . the ball in consequence trickling down to the Vauxhall end screen, there to be fielded by urchins and handed over reverentially to the bobby on duty . . . '

The account in Woolley's own autobiography is polite but pointed: 'It was rather a trying time for me, especially as it was my first Test innings . . . After my long wait it is perhaps not surprising that "Tibs" Cotter bowled me for 8.'

THE BOARD-ROOM BRAWL

In the last years before the First World War, neither country managed to field its strongest XI very often. England's selection for the 1909 series was battier than ever, partly because C.B. Fry's wife Beatrice insisted on sticking her battleaxe in. In the words of the cricket writer Denzil Batchelor, 'Sometimes she had not seen the players in action, but she appeared to have an instinct about their very names which reacted no less sensitively than a dowser's twig.'

> **'Come back and fight, you coward!'**
>
> Australia's chairman of selectors Peter McAlister after being decked by skipper Clem Hill during a selection meeting

England's method of picking teams may have been wrong-headed. It may even have 'touched the confines of lunacy', as *Wisden* memorably put it. But at least it did not leave blood on the carpet. That is literally what happened in Sydney in February 1912, when Australia's captain Clem Hill spent 20 minutes in a full-blown fistfight with Peter McAlister, his chairman of selectors.

This was more than just a disagreement over who should open the batting. McAlister was allied to Australia's Board of Control (BOC), which the players resented for its high-handedness and greed. He also had a reputation for bias, possibly stemming from his decision to pick himself on the 1909 tour of England. So when this selection meeting grew frosty, and McAlister told Hill he was 'the worst captain in living memory', the usually even-tempered Hill

Clem Hill was noted for being a fine exponent of the pull shot. He also had a pretty handy left hook, as he demonstrated on Peter McAlister, a widely despised chairman of selectors

replied: 'You've been asking for a punch all night.' With that, he leaned across the table and delivered one.

The fight raged around the room, which was on the third floor in Bull's Chambers. It ended when Hill tried to push McAlister out of the window, but BOC secretary Syd Smith managed to grab him by the coat-tails and hustle him away. In a Pythonesque conclusion, McAlister shouted 'Come back and fight, you coward!' from his prone position on the floor.

There was little chance of hushing the affair up. When the

Australian team arrived in Melbourne three days later, newspapers reported that McAlister had a cut nose, a bruise under the left eye and numerous scratches on his face. But public opinion inclined towards Hill. He received a variety of enthusiastic telegrams, ranging from 'Hip Hip Only regret blighter still living' to 'Congratulations self Armstrong bonzers you beauties.' Nobody likes a management spy, least of all in Australia.

Back on the field, England reclaimed the Ashes 4–1 that winter. They had a strong side, and some eccentric methods. The feared new-ball duo of Sydney Barnes and Frank Foster took a glass of champagne at every break in play, believing it to be a powerful restorative. Their success must have done wonders for French exports, but one cannot help wondering how they would have fared against a more united Australian side.

Relations with the BOC would get worse before they got better. Much of that 1911–12 season was spent wrangling over the team for England the following summer. A group of leading players,

1911–12: 5 TESTS
ENGLAND 4–1

S.F. BARNES (ENG.)   34 wkts at 22.88

J.B. HOBBS (ENG.)   662 runs at 82.75

Pelham Warner fell ill after the opening tour match, so J.W.H.T. Douglas led a triumphant England tour. Barnes and Frank Foster were unstoppable, taking 66 wickets between them. In the fourth Test at Melbourne, Hobbs and Rhodes shared an opening stand of 323 – the highest Ashes partnership until the advent of Bradman.

including Armstrong, Hill and Trumper, refused to go unless they were allowed to choose their own manager. As the board would not back down, none of the Big Six – as they were known – appeared in the Triangular Tournament of 1912. The final Test saw Syd Gregory's depleted side go down by 244 runs in the last Ashes encounter before the Great War.

1912: 3 TESTS
ENGLAND 1–0

J.B. HOBBS (ENG.) — 224 runs at 56.00

F.E. WOOLLEY (ENG.) — 99 runs at 24.75 & 10 wkts at 5.50

The combination of a wet summer and a weak South Africa put paid to this one-off experiment of a Triangular Tournament. England played Australia three times, but they had to add a fourth day to the final Test to get a result. Frank Woolley scored 66 runs and took 10 wickets in the match.

LAUNCH OF 'THE BIG SHIP'

Everything was different after 1918. More than 60 English first-class cricketers had died in the fighting, including Percy Jeeves, a whippy Warwickshire all-rounder who would surely have played for England. Still, Jeeves's surname would pass into the national consciousness by a different route. P.G. Wodehouse saw him play, and was inspired to a creative frame of mind. Armstrong, too, was different. Over four years without first-class cricket, his already enormous frame had expanded even further. One of his shirts from the period is preserved in the Melbourne Cricket Ground museum; it measures 96 centimetres by 85. Journalists and commentators dubbed him 'The Big Ship', though opponents might have queried that final consonant.

> **'If he failed to reach an edged ball, they would yell, "You big jellyfish" and coarser terms of endearment.'**
>
> Ray Robinson on
> Warwick Armstrong

Armstrong's size would earn him plenty of grief from the stands. The historian Ray Robinson wrote, 'If he failed to reach an edged ball, they would yell, "You big jellyfish" and coarser terms of endearment.' But no cricketer can ever have been more impervious to his audience. Armstrong's perspective

W.W. ARMSTRONG (AUS.) 464 runs at 77.33 & 9 wkts at 22.66

J.M. GREGORY (AUS.) 442 runs at 73.66 & 23 wkts at 24.17

Armstrong defied malaria and hostile administrators to lead his team to the first 5–0 whitewash in Ashes history. While England's bowling was underpowered, the Australians had Jack Gregory's pace and Arthur Mailey's googlies.

on barracking could have been summed up by Samuel Johnson's epigram: 'A fly, Sir, may sting a stately horse and make him wince; but one is but an insect, and the other is still a horse.'

The 1920–21 series was one long victory parade for Armstrong. He scored 464 runs, with three centuries, and wrapped up the second Test by taking four for 26. But still the administrators hated and feared him. Armstrong's biggest critic was Ernie Bean, the man who ran his own state cricket association of Victoria. If the two surnames happen to suggest a strong-armed champion, pestered by a small-minded, bean-counting official, the image would not be too far from the truth.

The obligatory flashpoint of 1920–21 came when Armstrong pulled out of Victoria's match against Sydney because of bruising inflicted by England's fast bowler Harry Howell. According to a team-mate, his legs looked 'like a futurist painting . . . a chaotic welter of clashing colour'. But Armstrong announced his decision

> **'You know, Fender, there is no man in England whose bowling I would rather face than yours; and there is no batsman in England I would rather bowl against either.'**
>
> MCC captain J.W.H.T. Douglas to his
> all-rounder Percy Fender before the
> 1920–21 Ashes series

to his peers rather than the team manager – a minor breach of protocol that Bean treated like a capital offence.

The fourth Test found Armstrong suffering from one of his periodic attacks of malaria, which he had contracted in Malaysia during the team's journey home in 1909. His usual method of self-medication was with whisky. According to Ray Robinson, he took a stiff dose when Australia lost their fifth wicket. Robinson's account continues: 'I heard later that as Armstrong walked in to bat, he saw among the sea of faces the countenance of Bean, wearing an expression that seemed to say "I've got him now!" The sight of the teetotaller, seemingly gloating, sobered Armstrong if he needed sobering . . . The punchline of the story was that when Armstrong came out Bean was drunk.'

Mr Bean could only respond with a veto on Roy Park, Armstrong's friend and protégé, who played at Melbourne and was dismissed by the only Test ball he ever faced. His wife dropped her knitting and missed his whole career.

DOUBLE-QUICK

When we look at Armstrong, we see not only the first modern cricketer but the first glimmer of modern cricket. There was more to his captaincy than sledging, gamesmanship and clashes with authority. He also invented the two-pronged pace attack, that staple of the 20th-century game.

> **'He runs along a sinister curve, lithe as a panther, his whole body moving like visible, dangerous music.'**
>
> Neville Cardus on Australian quick Ted McDonald

For cricket fans raised on Lillee and Thomson, or even Gough and Caddick, the new-ball pairing is an important building block of any team – perhaps *the* most important, given how many modern Tests are won by fast bowlers. But before the First World War, it was more conventional to open with a quick from one end and a slow from the other. The only seamers to hunt as a pair were England's wily Barnes and Foster in 1911–12.

Australian fast bowlers Jack Gregory and Ted McDonald were quite different. Why waste time working a batsman out, they reasoned, when you can knock him out instead? This was the fate that befell Ernest Tyldesley at Trent Bridge in 1921, courtesy of a Jack Gregory bouncer. To add insult to injury, the ball then rebounded onto his stumps. Ernest's more famous brother, J.T. Tyldesley, scolded him afterwards: 'Get to the off side of the ball whenever you hook, then, if you miss it, it passes harmlessly over the left shoulder.'

Gregory, appropriately enough, had served in the artillery corps during the First World War, and was spotted by Pelham Warner during a wartime match against the Red Cross. He was a big man, some 6ft 3in tall, with an untutored method: he simply

Jack Gregory:
the young Wally
Hammond
wrote that he
had 'cultivated
a fearsome stare
and gave me the
treatment. With
knees shaking
and hands
trembling,
I was relieved
when he bowled
me first ball'

ran in as fast as he could, leapt as high as he could, and let the ball go with all the force he could muster.

McDonald was subtler. A tall but slight figure, he had a chest-on action and a deceptive rhythm. In Neville Cardus's words 'he runs along a sinister curve, lithe as a panther, his whole body moving like visible, dangerous music'. Together, these two must have been a little like facing Colin Croft and Michael Holding, two great West Indian fast bowlers of the 1970s and 1980s – the first all sound and fury, the other known as 'Whispering Death'.

The roll-call of casualties was a long one, at least by the standards of the day: Cambridge University's Hubert Ashton retired after a blow on the hand, Lancashire's J.R. Barnes took a ball to the head, and Essex's Percy Perrin was laid low by a whack in the

'What's this damnable side of picnickers they've sent me?'

J.W.H.T. Douglas reacts to his England side for the Lord's Test, 1921

stomach. England's captain J.W.H.T. Douglas (his multiple initials and stubborn batting style inspired the Australians to dub him 'Johnny Won't Hit Today') was hardly lacking in physical courage. He had won gold as a middleweight at the 1908 Olympics. But there was little he could do to halt Armstrong's army.

Douglas's last Ashes Test in charge – and seventh consecutive defeat – came in the second Test at Lord's. It started badly: the selection of four debutants prompted him to exclaim: 'What's this damnable side of picnickers they've sent me?' Then it got worse. One of those debutants, Johnny Evans, was 'so nervous that he could hardly hold his bat, while his knees were literally knocking together', according to team-mate Lionel Tennyson. 'I endeavoured to put some heart into him by a few timely words when I joined him at the wicket, but it was useless; his nerve was gone, and the first straight ball was enough for him.' Since the hapless Evans had escaped from a German POW camp during the War, one might have expected a little more bravado.

Tennyson, by contrast, was England's hero of the resistance. He stood firm in the second innings, scoring an unbeaten 74, despite the repeated blows inflicted by the enemy. By the next Test, he had been appointed England captain.

AN OFFICER AND A GAMESMAN

Lionel Tennyson could almost have wandered out
of an episode of *Blackadder Goes Forth*. He was a
soldier and an aristocrat, a man who employed a
chauffeur to drive the 80 yards between his Jermyn
Street flat and White's, his favourite club. He wrote
poetry too: his grandfather was the poet laureate,
Alfred Lord Tennyson, whom he claimed to
remember as 'a beard at the foot of the bed'.

Contemporary photographs reveal a classic British bulldog.
Tennyson learned cricket on Eton's playing fields and leadership
on the French battlefields. His life, according to the novelist A.A.
Thomson, 'consisted of one long cavalry charge'.

Tennyson showed his officer-class contempt for pain during the
third Test at Leeds. Fielding a firm shot, he split the webbing of his
left hand. Then, when his time came to bat, he wrapped the injured
hand in a wire basket, picked up a youth's bat, and set about driving
Gregory and McDonald down the ground like a right-handed
squash player. The result was 62 out of an 88-run stand with
Douglas, who presumably wasn't hitting that day.

Tennyson formed an unlikely friendship with Armstrong,
describing him as 'a mountain of geniality'. But at Old Trafford, he
was on the end of one of Armstrong's most ingenious tricks. England
were already 3–0 down by this stage and a first-day washout hardly
helped their cause. At 5.50pm on the second day, Tennyson declared
England's first innings closed at 341 for four, only to be confronted by
Armstrong and a copy of *Wisden*. A scholarly discussion of the Laws
ensued. According to Armstrong, the loss of the first day meant that

Lionel Tennyson received the news of his call-up for the 1921 Lord's Test during a late-night drinking session at the Embassy Club in Bond Street. Tennyson bet his chums £50 he'd make a half-century, and went on to score a heroic 74 in a losing cause

the Test had become a two-day game (Law 55). And as declarations in two-day games were not permitted after a certain cut-off point, Tennyson's declaration was illegal (Law 54).

The teams trooped back out, whereupon Armstrong took advantage of the confusion to bowl a second consecutive over (so breaking Law 14). That seemed far more in character. In fact, it was not Armstrong who had spotted the legal loophole, but Australia's 43-year-old wicketkeeper Hanson Carter. Despite the presence of multiple England captains in the pavilion, the home side were left floundering.

In those days Tests in England only lasted three days, in contrast to Australia's 'timeless' matches, so a couple of showers were usually terminal. The last game of the 1921 series suffered from more delays, prompting hundreds of angry fans to invade the field and gather under the pavilion balcony, shouting:

'Arthur, you've been using resin. I'll report you to the umpires.' 'You've been lifting the seam, Johnny.'
Ball-tampering, 1920s style: Australia's Arthur Mailey and England's J.W.H.T. Douglas

'Be sportsmen!', 'Play up!', and 'Windy!' The contest became so futile that, on his final day of Test cricket, Armstrong was reported to have grabbed a newspaper blowing across the ground and scanned the sports page. He later claimed that he 'wanted to see who we were playing'.

So ended Armstrong's undefeated reign as Australian captain: eight successive wins followed by two nose-thumbing draws. He represented a tipping-point in cricket history, the moment when the fair play of the Golden Age segued into something far tougher and more pragmatic. His team intimidated the opposition, both with their fast bowlers and their sheer self-assurance. Melbourne's *Herald* paid tribute to 'Their easy confident bearing, their smiling exchanges of badinage . . . here is a team that is pretty sure of itself.' The banter, the body language, the attitude – none of it would feel out of place today. When today's coaches tell their fielders that 11 men should be able to out-psych two, they are only following in Armstrong's broad wake.

1921: 5 TESTS
AUSTRALIA 3–0

J.M. GREGORY (AUS.)   19 wkts at 29.05

E.A. McDONALD (AUS.)   27 wkts at 24.74

Ted McDonald joined Gregory in the fastest new-ball pairing the game had ever seen. They extended Australia's winning sequence to eight Tests, before rain and Phil Mead's obstinate batting reduced the last two games to stalemate. England broke their 1909 record by fielding 30 players in the series.

'PRAY GOD, NO PROFESSIONAL SHALL CAPTAIN ENGLAND'

If Armstrong came from Mars, Jack Hobbs was a peace-loving Venusian. His lack of ego made him almost unique among great batsmen (the one other exception being Trumper). Wilfred Rhodes, discussing his astonishing record of 197 centuries, once claimed: 'He could have made 397 if he'd wanted but when Surrey were going well he used to throw it away – give his wicket to one of his old pals, hit up a catch and go out laughing.'

Hobbs was the pre-eminent figure in Ashes cricket for the mid to late 1920s. This may explain why it was a calm and law-abiding era, a lull between the banditry that went before and the bloodshed that followed. In more enlightened times, he would have been made captain, but he was a gentleman in every sense save the one that mattered to the selectors. So Hobbs served under a succession of inferior cricketers. He did get one chance as a stand-in during the fourth Test of 1926, after Arthur Carr went down with tonsillitis on the first evening. It was a historic moment; the only other professional to lead England against Australia had been Arthur Shrewsbury in 1886–87. But Carr was unimpressed.

'If I may say so, I thought [Hobbs] was a rotten captain. But then, I am afraid, most pros are not much good at the job.'

This was very much the thinking of the day. Only a couple of months earlier, Lord Hawke had addressed the Yorkshire members with his famous remark: 'Pray God, no professional shall captain England.' Cricket's class divide was so embedded that few 'players' even aspired to a position of authority. The Yorkshire professional Herbert Sutcliffe turned down the county captaincy, while Arthur Mailey wrote: 'Although Jack did have the honour of captaining England, he felt at the time like the best man who was asked to become a bigamist because the groom failed to appear.'

The distinction between gentlemen and players was reinforced by separate dressing-rooms. On the scorecard, they could be distinguished by the position of the initials: amateurs before the surname, professionals after. As late as 1949, this remained a big enough deal for the Lord's tannoy to announce: 'F.J. Titmus should, of course, read Titmus F.J.'

> **'I thought [Hobbs] was a rotten captain. But then, I am afraid, most pros are not much good at the job.'**
>
> England captain Arthur Carr, an amateur

Hobbs and Sutcliffe made ideal serfs, defying opposition bowlers while deferring to their own feudal overlords. In 1924–25, their opening partnership was the only thing that came close to worrying Australia's sphinx-like captain, Herbie Collins. Not even a tight finish at Adelaide could disturb Collins's inscrutable cool. With 27 runs needed at stumps on the fifth evening, the anxious batsmen had an early night, while the Australians played gramophone records till dawn, then staggered out and knocked over the last two wickets.

That final morning featured an early instance of attempted match-fixing. Before Australia left for the ground, Collins was approached by a well-upholstered chap with a cigar. After a brief chat, he remarked to Arthur Mailey: 'This fellow says it's worth a hundred quid if we lose the match. Let's throw him downstairs.' The entrepreneur made a hasty exit; he must have expected Collins, a bookmaker by trade, to be more receptive.

Jack Hobbs and Herbert Sutcliffe, England's greatest opening pair. John Arlott wrote of Hobbs, 'The Master: records prove the title good: / Yet figures fail you, for they cannot say / How many men whose names you never knew / Are proud to tell their sons they saw you play'

1924–25: 5 TESTS
AUSTRALIA 4–1

H. SUTCLIFFE (ENG.) | 734 runs at 81.55

M.W. TATE (ENG.) | 38 wkts at 23.21

The outstanding individual feats were English, but Australia's teamwork took the spoils. Leg-spinner Clarrie Grimmett, the first man to bowl the flipper, was introduced in the final Test and took 11 for 82.

1926: 5 TESTS
ENGLAND 1–0

J.B. HOBBS (ENG.) | **486 runs at 81.00**

M.W. TATE (ENG.) | **13 wkts at 29.84**

England won the Ashes back for the first time in 14 years. The weather was just as bad as in that 1912 summer, and the final Test had to be extended to a fourth day. Australia led by 22 on first innings, then a Hobbs–Sutcliffe special took the game away.

Back in England, 1925 was to be Hobbs's year. For four weeks, between 20 July and 17 August, the only question in sport was when he would score his next century, and so equal W.G. Grace's long-standing record of 126 first-class hundreds. His dismissal for 54 on bank holiday Monday prompted the somewhat ironic headline: 'Hobbs fails again.' When he finally reached three figures at Taunton, then added a 127th century the very next day, a French newspaper reported that he had surpassed even Grace's feat of hitting a ball into the face of Big Ben. Hobbs, a teetotaller, celebrated with a glass of ginger beer.

THE INTEMPERANCE SOCIETY

The 1920s were a great decade for hedonism, if you were able to afford it. And many amateur cricketers could. Arthur Carr certainly had a taste for beer and cocktails, which may have cut short his career as England captain. 'The devil of it is that if you drink at all people are so apt to exaggerate about you,' he complained in his chippy autobiography, *Cricket With The Lid Off*.

Exaggeration may not have been strictly necessary. Only four pages later, Carr relates 'the historic occasion on which, after having had a few, I was driving two of the Notts team back home at a fast pace. One of the two ... went to sleep and fell off the back of the car and I and the other did not know he was missing until an efficient young gentleman in blue stopped us and suggested that I and my companion . . . should accompany him to the station. When we got there I was invited to say, "Sister Susie's sewing shirts for soldiers."'

Carr described Percy Chapman, his successor as England captain, as 'the always-ready-to-be-matey-and-social Percy'. His choice of expression is every bit as euphemistic as that staple of the obituary page: 'Mr Smith was a confirmed bachelor.' When Carr had his attack of tonsillitis, the 26-year-old Chapman was pressed into service as twelfth man, despite having drunk a gutful of ale the previous night. He later claimed that the summons had been one

A.P.F. (Percy) Chapman: according to his obituary in *The Cricketer*, he brought 'his own sparkling brand of cricket to the first-class game'. He liked a spot of bubbly in the dressing-room too

of the worst experiences of his young life. But when the team was announced for the next Test, the substitute suddenly found himself in charge.

Chapman turned out to be a revelation. He led England to seven successive Test victories, a feat that went unequalled until 2004. The first three wins were a doddle – candy taken from the inaugural West Indian tourists – but the next four had to be chiselled out against the 1928–29 Australians. One of the finest fielders of his day, Chapman set the tone for that Ashes series with a blinding take off the fourth ball of Larwood's first over. According to Percy Fender, 'It flew knee high wide of Chapman's left hand in the gully, and the latter made a pace towards it and held on to it with his left arm fully extended. I don't think I have ever seen a better catch and not half-a-dozen so good.'

Mysteriously, Chapman stood down for the final Test. He claimed to have 'flu, though some believe he was embarrassed

'Wally, well, yes – he liked a shag!'

Eddie Paynter on the great Wally Hammond

about his batting form, and others reckon he was just plain drunk. While he would lead England another nine times, his heyday was at an end, and on retirement he unwisely accepted a post as a rep for a whisky company. Years later, a group of Sussex colts were training at Hove when their coach, Patsy Hendren, suddenly vanished into a nearby tent. At that moment, a huge red-faced drunk lurched through their midst. When Hendren reappeared, he explained that he couldn't bear to see Percy Chapman, the greatest captain he ever served under, in such a terrible state.

Chapman's star turn on that 1928–29 tour was Wally Hammond, another enthusiastic drinker. But Hammond's real addiction was to sex. He was the Hugh Hefner of English cricket, a man who thought nothing of telling his landlord: 'If I tilt [the bedroom mirror] at the right angle, I can see your wife undressing.' David Foot's biography, *Wally Hammond: The Reasons Why*, recounts the story of how he used to keep two or three mistresses on the go, while neglecting his depressed and alcoholic wife. Foot also drew this memorable quote from Eddie Paynter: 'Wally, well, yes – he liked a shag!'

After his first tour, to the West Indies in 1926, Hammond returned home looking emaciated. He had a fever and an inflamed leg. The condition was serious enough to send him into a nursing-home for several months while doctors repeatedly lanced a septic swelling in the lymph glands around the groin. In retrospect, it is clear that he was suffering from syphilis. Hammond's explanation was that he had been bitten by a mosquito during the team's stay in British Guiana, and had contracted blood poisoning as a result. This is another first-class euphemism. Hammond may have been bitten in British Guiana. He may even have been bitten in the groin. But not, it seems, by a mosquito.

JEALOUS RIVALS

That was far from being the end for Hammond, who made it to 62 before a heart attack finally did for him. *Wisden* published a typically pompous obituary. 'The judgment of cricket history is that the greatest batsmen the game has known are – in order of appearance, only – W.G. Grace, Jack Hobbs, Walter Hammond and Don Bradman.'

Hammond's biggest obsession, apart from his genitals, was his position in this exalted pecking order. He wanted the palace on top of Mount Olympus, and bugger the bloke next door. So it was just his luck that his Test career coincided almost exactly with Bradman's, the one player good enough to look down on him. Every century Bradman scored took another chip out of Hammond's self-esteem.

Hammond's relationship with Bradman was one of unrequited envy. The Don did not bother about rivals: he always knew he had top billing. Poor Hammond was cast as his eternal understudy. They arrived on stage together, during England's 1928–29 tour, and took their last bow in consecutive series after the Second World War.

That first encounter was the only one that went England's way. Hammond piled up 905 runs, smashing Sutcliffe's Ashes record of 734. Everyone who saw him agreed that he was a thrilling player to watch, particularly when driving through the off-side. But his technique was essentially orthodox. Bradman, with his bottom-handed grip and all-purpose pull-shot, broke conventions as well as bowlers' hearts.

> **'The greatest player we shall ever see – but a funny bugger.'**
> **Anon. Gloucestershire team-mate on Wally Hammond**

It remains a historical curiosity that Australia lost Bradman's first Test by 675 runs – the highest figure ever recorded. He batted down the order,

Two immortals: Don Bradman leads the way,
and Wally Hammond's expression suggests
that he knows it only too well

Wally Hammond broke all the batting records in the book. He scored four centuries, including 251 and 200 in successive innings. But Don Bradman, Hammond's future nemesis, put down a marker of his own.

made 18 and 1, and was then dropped for the only time in his career. Hammond, by contrast, scored a monumental 251. Clearly established as the world's leading cricketer, he is unlikely to have seen the frail country boy from Bowral, New South Wales, as a future threat. His relaxed state of mind was revealed by Ben Travers, an English playwright, who wrote that every time the players came off the field, Hammond would come to see him in the stands, borrow his field glasses, and sit there scanning the Ladies' Enclosure.

Bradman came back, of course. In the third match of the series, aged 20, he became the youngest man to score a Test hundred. Still, when Australia's selectors sat down at the end of the summer, they probably saw 19-year-old Archie Jackson – who broke that record with 164 in the very next match – as the better prospect. Jackson was a sublimely elegant player, far more classical in his style than the almost robotic Bradman. But he died of tuberculosis just four years later, leaving one man to hog the limelight for the next couple of decades.

DON'S DELIGHT:

THE BRADMAN ERA:

1930–1948

'I think the Don was too good,' wrote Hobbs of Bradman.
'I do not think we want to see another one quite like him.
I do not think we ever shall'

BRADMAN'S SUMMER OF SUMMITS

Bradman was a walking anomaly. Performance levels in any field can usually be plotted on a bell curve, with most people bunched together around the middle and a few exceptional cases strung out at either end. So how, in a sport with millions of participants, did one player end up with a Test average almost 40 runs higher than the next man?

Bradman was not just the most freakish individual in cricket; he was the most freakish individual in sport. Men like Pelé, Jack Nicklaus, Jansher Khan and Roger Federer could all claim to have dominated their own disciplines, but Bradman reinvented his. As Disraeli once said of Gladstone, he had not a single redeeming defect.

If Bradman was the greatest batsman who ever lived, then 1930 was his greatest season, and Lord's the venue for his greatest innings. It took him just under three sessions to compile 254, then the highest score by an Australian, without a hint of a chance. In that Test, Bradman came as near to omnipotence as any mortal can. As he later wrote, 'Practically without exception every ball went where it was intended to go, even the one from which I was dismissed, but the latter went slightly up in the air and Percy Chapman with a miraculous piece of work held the catch.'

'Bloody Bradman!'
An exasperated Wally Hammond

Just 5ft 7in tall, and delicately built, Bradman was lighter on his feet than Peter Pan. Facing his very first ball at Lord's, he ran down the pitch and drove to long-off on the full. This daring sortie sent a withering message to the opposition; it was as if a tennis player had come forward to receive serve at the net. Neville Cardus wrote that it was 'an impertinent crack . . . when he finished the stroke he was close enough to J.C. White to see the look of astonishment on the bowler's face'.

In the next Test at Leeds, Bradman broke his own record again. This time he struck 334, 309 of them in a day. Hammond, by contrast, managed just 306 in the whole series. He was beginning to understand how Salieri must have felt about Mozart. In quiet moments at Bristol, his Gloucestershire team-mates could hear him burst out: 'Bloody Bradman!'

Not everyone in the tourists' camp was overjoyed to have this mechanical imp in their midst. After all, Ashes cricket was supposed to pit Australia against England, not one man against

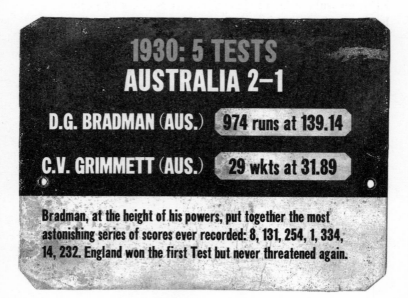

1930: 5 TESTS
AUSTRALIA 2–1

D.G. BRADMAN (AUS.) 974 runs at 139.14

C.V. GRIMMETT (AUS.) 29 wkts at 31.89

Bradman, at the height of his powers, put together the most astonishing series of scores ever recorded: 8, 131, 254, 1, 334, 14, 232. England won the first Test but never threatened again.

eleven. Jack Hobbs described Bradman as 'a team in himself', and at times, Bradman himself seemed to believe it. Such tensions could have been defused if only Bradman had been a clubbable sort of fellow. But he was nothing of the sort. At the end of a day's play, he would bypass the bar and head straight to his room, where he listened to music and wrote letters to his wife. 'Who's the stranger?' was a regular quip among the team.

Even when a soap magnate presented him with a £1,000 reward for his triple-hundred, there was not a sniff of a round of drinks. When an exasperated colleague suggested that he should spend some of the money on 'a dinner for the boys', he replied: 'If I gave you fellows a dinner every night from now until we got home to Australia you would only say what a fool I am.'

When Bradman finally returned home, 974 runs to the good, some of his fellow tourists made light of his achievements. 'We could have played any team without Don Bradman, but we could not play the blind school without [leg-spinner] Clarrie Grimmett,' said Vic Richardson, somewhat absurdly. A more damning verdict came from the anonymous player who suggested that Bradman 'is the best batsman in the world, but that is where he finishes. He did not spend twopence during the tour.' For all his unique gifts, Bradman's team-mates clearly thought him as tight as two coats of paint.

> **'Bradman didn't break my heart in 1930, he just made me very, very tired.'**
> **England fast bowler Harold Larwood**

DOUGLAS JARDINE: MADE IN SCOTLAND FROM GIRDERS

'Who breaks a butterfly on a wheel?' asked the 18th-century poet Alexander Pope. He found his answer in Douglas Jardine, a thin-lipped, cold-eyed amateur who could have been bred for the purpose. Jardine was appointed England captain in July 1931. His mission, as he chose to accept it, was to put an end to Bradman's run-spree.

> **'He might well win us the Ashes, but he might lose us a Dominion.'**
> **Douglas Jardine's cricket master at Winchester**

From the way Jardine carried himself, anyone would have thought he was a high-ranking member of the aristocracy – a minor royal at least. In fact, he was born in Bombay, in India, into a dynasty of well-heeled Scottish lawyers. At the age of nine he was sent to live with his Aunt Kitty in a forbidding country house near St Andrews. It was the sort of remote mansion where celluloid villains brood over their plans for world domination. And no doubt the young Jardine did plenty of brooding of his own.

Jardine's character traits were well established by the time he

Haughty and distant, Douglas Jardine was everything that Australians hated about the old country. His Harlequin cap said it all

reached Winchester College. He was arrogant, egotistical, and about as popular with his class-mates as a needle in an inflatable lifeboat. He once celebrated winning the school's inter-house competition by pinning up an unconventional team sheet. 'Cook House: D.R. Jardine, W.M. Leggatt. The following might have been included had they not been unable to bat or bowl, or even to field . . . ' One can only imagine what he would have said if they had lost.

There is a keen irony in the fact that Winchester's headmaster at the time was Montague Rendall, the man who coined the BBC's motto: 'Nation shall speak peace unto nation'. Such Reithian sentiments rang hollow when Jardine's brutal 'Bodyline' tactics were turning five-and-a-half ounces of cork and leather into a deadly weapon. Indeed, the rumpus caused by Bodyline came within an ace of capsizing Anglo-Australian relations.

The teenage Jardine clearly left a strong impression on his cricket master, Rockley Wilson. When he was appointed England

'All Australians are uneducated, and an unruly mob.'
Douglas Jardine

> **'He is a queer fellow. When he sees a cricket ground with an Australian on it, he goes mad.'**
>
> Pelham Warner on Jardine

captain, a journalist asked Wilson to rate his prospects. The reply was almost supernaturally prescient: 'He might well win us the Ashes, but he might lose us a Dominion.'

Jardine's obsession with the Ashes made Captain Ahab look like a man on a pleasure cruise. Of course all sportsmen want to win, that is the nature of the beast, but there was a personal element to this crusade. Despite his Scottish roots, Jardine was determined to prove England's moral and cultural superiority through the medium of sport. And his zeal was only sharpened by the fact that, in his eyes, Australia was a nation of moustachioed neanderthals. 'All Australians are uneducated, and an unruly mob,' he remarked to one close fielder during the 1928–29 tour.

Jack Fingleton, one of Jardine's opponents in the Bodyline series, believed that his anti-Australian bias could be traced all the way back to 1921. That was the year when the Australians' tour match against Oxford University had to be wound up in two days, leaving the 20-year-old Jardine stranded on 96 not out. It is an interesting theory, but a little like suggesting that Tom chased Jerry because he had been scarred by a tough upbringing. Maybe Warwick Armstrong should have had the decency to stay on the field for another couple of overs. But it would have made no difference. Jardine and Australia were made to despise each other; they were always going to be at loggerheads. As Pelham Warner wrote in 1934: 'He is a queer fellow. When he sees a cricket ground with an Australian on it, he goes mad.'

'I'VE GOT IT, HE'S YELLOW!'

Jardine's first priority was to crack the Enigma code: how to get Bradman out. He took his cue from the lines written by Pelham Warner: 'England must evolve a new type of bowler and develop fresh ideas, strategy and tactics to curb his almost uncanny skill.'

In an early example of video analysis, Jardine spent hours studying film from the 1930 series. Reel after reel revealed nothing but the dispiriting sight of Bradman tap-dancing down the pitch and belting the ball to the boundary. Even the art of field-placing seemed irrelevant, as Bradman never hit the ball in the air. He struck two sixes on the entire 1930 tour, and one of those was off a no-ball.

Finally, as the projector clicked round to the final Test at The Oval, Jardine let out a yell: 'I've got it, he's yellow!' The images showed Harold Larwood, England's fastest bowler, making the ball lift awkwardly on a drying pitch. Archie Jackson moved bravely into line and took some terrible blows, including one under the heart that almost made him physically sick. Bradman, by contrast, kept his body well out of the way. He went on to score 232, but that was not the point. Jardine was convinced that he had seen the great man flinch.

An unusual company sat down to dine at the Piccadilly Grill Rooms in August 1932. Two of the four men

> 'Some challenged, like Trumper; some charmed, like Ranjitsinhji; Bradman devastated – deliberately, coldly, ruthlessly.'
>
> J.M. Kilburn

**Harold Larwood: at his liveliest after a couple of lunchtime pints.
'I never bowled to injure a man. Frighten them, intimidate them – yes'**

were amateurs: the monkish Jardine and the rakish Arthur Carr,
captain of Nottinghamshire. The other two made up Carr's new-
ball attack at Trent Bridge: Bill Voce, a barrel-chested left-arm
quick, and Larwood himself, the man whose extreme pace made
Bodyline possible.

Little time was devoted to discussing the menu and wine list.
Even the food lay largely untouched on the plates. It was Bradman
they had come to dissect. 'I told Jardine I thought Bradman had
flinched and he said he knew that,' Larwood wrote. 'Finally Jardine

'You cannot be a great fast bowler on a bottle of ginger-pop.'

Larwood's Nottinghamshire captain, Arthur Carr

asked me if I thought I could bowl on the leg stump making the ball come up into the body all the time so that Bradman had to play his shots to leg. "Yes, I think that can be done," I said. "It's better to rely on speed and accuracy than anything else when bowling to Bradman because he murders any loose stuff."'

It was that very speed and accuracy, channelled through Larwood's human catapult, which made Bodyline effective. Just 5ft 9in but supremely athletic, Larwood left school at 13 to work in the mines, where he chiselled away at seams of coal with a pick-axe. It was a tough apprenticeship but it gave him both strength and motive: any man would have bowled until his feet bled to escape a life like that.

The young Larwood was almost touchingly naïve. His first trip to London took him to the lobby of a smart West End hotel, where he turned to a team-mate and breathed: 'Are *all* these women for hire?' But Carr had a method of dealing with unworldly fast bowlers: he weaned them onto beer. His contention was: 'You cannot be a great fast bowler on a bottle of ginger-pop.' Soon Larwood was felling batsmen across the country, especially in the early afternoon. County cricketers soon discovered that he was at his fiercest just after a couple of lunchtime pints.

THE ONSLAUGHT BEGINS

On 17 September 1932, England's tourists set off for Australia with malice aforethought. Jardine spent the month-long journey preaching like a fundamentalist. The only way to beat the Aussies, he kept repeating, was to hate them. When the boat docked, the first thing Jardine did was to reject a gift of a bottle of Scotch for each man of the team. The second was to turn down the *Sydney Sun*'s request for team information with the words: 'What damned rot!' This England party had not come to enjoy themselves, nor to make friends. They had come to beat Bradman in his own back-yard.

'What damned rot!'

Jardine rejects an Australian press request for team information, 1932

Even before the tourists took the field for the first time, Bradman's antennae were quivering. (His knees would shortly follow.) In the words of his team-mate, Jack Fingleton, he 'saw something most unprecedented in that four of [England's] bowlers, Larwood, Allen, Voce and Bowes, were fast bowlers . . . It meant only one thing to Bradman. They were after his batting skin.'

Jardine kept his hand shielded until the final two warm-up matches, against an Australian XI and New South Wales. Then the Bodyline barrage began. Its potency was immediately obvious.

Passage to infamy: even on the boat to Australia, Jardine
was already steeling his troops for the assault to come

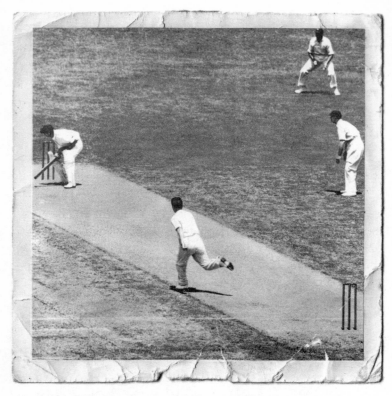

Jack Fingleton ducks a Larwood bouncer: note the short-leg and leg-gully, lurking in readiness for the unwary fend

Bradman started to bat in ways that would have seen any ordinary player drummed out of the team. He drew back to cut off the stumps and was bowled. He sat down to avoid a bouncer, but the ball hit the back of his bat and ricocheted to mid-on.

Some historians believe that even at this late stage, Jardine had not fully made up his mind to go with Bodyline. But when Bradman was bowled by Voce in the final state match, taking evasive action to a ball that hit his middle stump, there could be no doubt. This was batting from the Phil Tufnell handbook. According to Fingleton it was 'the most un-Bradmanlike happening of his entire career'.

Fingleton himself carried his bat for a brilliant unbeaten 119 in the first innings, defying one of Voce's most vicious spells. Larwood would later call him 'the most courageous man I ever bowled to'. Fingleton was also a first-rate reporter, and no one has ever matched his description of Bodyline in action:

'Voce bowled Bradman, but for the main purpose the stumps were intended to serve, they could well have been left in the pavilion. Most of Voce's deliveries, if they did not meet a New South Wales rib in transit, cleared the leg stump, or a space outside the leg stump, by feet . . . For a time several members of the English leg-side trap either offered apologies when a batsman was hit or gave a rubbing palm in solace; but a continuation of such courtesies would, in the circumstances, have been hypocritical and embarrassing to the giver and receiver alike. The batsman was later left to do his own rubbing in the privacy of his imprecations.'

Fingleton knew he should have been delighted by his innings. But 'there was, on the contrary, no wild thrill about it. I was conscious of a hurt, and it was not because of the physical pummelling I had taken from Voce. It was the consciousness of a crashed ideal.'

EVASIVE ACTION

Like most achievements in journalism, the invention of the term 'Bodyline' came about by accident. The *Melbourne Herald* reporter Hugh Buggy was filing his copy by telegraph from Sydney. After his first reference to 'bowling on the line of the body', he reverted to cost-cutting shorthand: 'Voce was hit for six, again bodyline bowling.' Thus it has been known ever since.

Buggy wrote his historic report on 2 December, the first day of the Test series. And Stan McCabe was the man biffing Voce for six. He clearly knew what to expect; on his way out to bat, he turned to his watching father and said, 'If I happen to get hit out there, keep Mum from jumping the fence and laying into those Pommy bowlers.'

Mrs McCabe needn't have worried. Her son stood up to the bouncers in every sense, meeting the ball head-on with a fusillade of hooks and pulls. He made an unforgettable 187 not out in just four hours, threading the ball through the leg-side cordon like an old sea-dog navigating a reef. The crowd were exultant, believing that McCabe's innings had spiked Jardine's guns. But McCabe himself knew better. He had been lucky, he said, so lucky that he did not believe he could produce the same results again. And so it proved.

> **'If I happen to get hit out there, keep Mum from jumping the fence and laying into those Pommy bowlers.'**
> Stan McCabe

Larwood took five for 28 in the second innings, leaving England just one run to win.

And what of Bradman? You might well ask. Almost unbelievably, Australia's champion had ruled himself out of the first Test on grounds of ill health. At the time, this must have

Even Homer nods: Bradman bottom-edges his first ball of the Bodyline series — a Bill Bowes long-hop — onto his stumps

seemed like a terrible anti-climax. Had Jardine schemed his way halfway around the world for nothing? No: Bradman took himself off to the seaside, then returned, apparently refreshed, for the second Test at Melbourne. For Australia's cricket-lovers, it must have been like that moment in every cop movie where the hero gets taken off the case. Now the tension was building. Could Bradman apprehend the culprit in the final reel?

Bradman's first ball of the series was a moment of pure theatre. Bill Bowes began his long, lumbering run, but the noise from the crowd was such that he had to stop twice on the way in. Then, finally, came the ball: short of a length, but gentle in pace — a custard pie, by comparison with one of Larwood's exocets. Bradman stepped across, aimed a pull-shot at midwicket, and bottom-edged the ball into the leg stump. It was the first golden duck of his Test career.

In the second innings, Bradman made amends with an unbeaten 103 — his only hundred of the series, and a match-winning hundred at that. But sport is a fickle mistress: within a few years, people had forgotten his hundred. They never forgot the golden duck.

THE BATTLE OF ADELAIDE

The most famous words in Ashes history, barring Brooks's obituary notice, are probably those spoken by Bill Woodfull in the Adelaide Oval dressing-room during the third Test. 'There are two teams out there on the oval,' he said. 'One is playing cricket, the other is not.'

Woodfull was lying on a massage table at the time. Less than an hour earlier, he had been hit over the heart by Larwood, who was making terrifying use of the liveliest strip of turf this side of the Triffids. While the blow clearly hurt, it was the reaction that really rankled. 'Well bowled, Harold,' exclaimed Jardine in a stentorian voice, intended mainly for the ears of Bradman at the other end.

Woodfull had some brief respite, as it was the last ball of Larwood's over. But when he faced up again, Jardine swung the field round to the leg-side – the signal for a full-scale Bodyline bombardment. Both captain and bowler have since claimed that the move was not intended to be hostile; Larwood just happened to be making the ball swing in. But the crowd were outraged. They jeered, hooted, and counted Larwood out – which is to say they shouted: 'One, two, three, four, five, six, seven, eight, nine, out YOU BASTARD!'

According to Arthur Carr, this was precisely the worst thing they could have done. 'The Australian crowds and newspapers played right into the hands of Larwood,' he wrote. 'They got his back up, made him angry and determined – and when you do that . . .

> **'Well bowled, Harold.'**
> Jardine to Larwood after the English paceman had hit Australia's captain over the heart

Bill Woodfull takes a Larwood thunderbolt over the heart, prompting
Jardine to roar 'Well bowled, Harold', and switch his fielders into
Bodyline positions for the next ball

you add to his effectiveness.' Eventually the fielders took up their
new positions and Larwood set off on the silky, gliding run that
had earned him the sobriquet 'murder on tip-toe'. The next ball
was faster than anything that had gone before, and knocked the bat
clean out of Woodfull's hands. Now the heckling went up another
notch; Larwood might as well have been strangling Skippy the
Bush Kangaroo.

In his autobiography, Arthur Mailey described the view from
Australia's dressing-room. 'Although the crowd in Adelaide is
probably the best behaved in Australia, I did think that on this
occasion the place would be torn down. What did Jardine do
about it? In the midst of all the noise and turmoil he walked away
from his fielding position close to the wicket and stationed himself
in the outfield where the din was at its worst . . . He was certainly
going out of his way to court trouble.'

'One, two, three, four, five, six, seven, eight, nine, out YOU BASTARD!'
Anti-Larwood Australian crowd chant

Bowled by Gubby Allen, Woodfull had barely taken up his position on the massage table when England's toffee-nosed management duo Pelham Warner and R.C.N. ('Dick') Palairet came creeping in to offer weasel words of sympathy. Woodfull then made his great pronouncement, concluding crushingly: 'The game is too good to be spoiled. It is time some people got out of it. Good afternoon.'

For an upstanding chap like Warner, this was a rum sort of pickle. A sporting moralist from the school of Lord Harris, he was a great one for spouting high-minded sentiments. But when decisive action was needed, as on this tour, he was equally good at keeping his head down. His parting shot to Woodfull was typically evasive: 'Apart from all that [i.e. all that pesky intimidation and violence stuff], we most sincerely hope you are not too badly hurt.' Sir Pelham Warner was knighted in 1937, presumably for services to humbug.

> **'There are two teams out there on the oval. One is playing cricket, the other is not.'**
> Australian captain W.M. Woodfull to England manager Pelham Warner

FIRST BLOOD

Bodyline's most infamous hour was still to come.
After a break for the Sabbath, the match restarted
on Monday with a police guard stationed around
the boundary. Thus Warner's 1904 prediction
(see page 57) had come to pass. Early that
afternoon, Australia's wicketkeeper Bert Oldfield
was entrenching himself for a long rearguard action
when he attempted a hook at Larwood. The ball
cannoned off the top-edge and into his skull.
At once Oldfield dropped his bat and collapsed,
clutching one hand to the wound.

**'If one man jumps
the fence the whole
mob will go for us.'**
Larwood fears for his safety
after hitting Oldfield
on the head

It was the moment Jardine's
critics had been waiting for:
incontrovertible proof that Bodyline
could turn an honourable game
into a threat to life and limb. The
crowd's dander was up again, to
the point where even Larwood was
alarmed. '"If anybody fires a pistol
they'll lynch us," I thought. "If one
man jumps the fence the whole mob will go for us."'

In Sydney, the fans would have vaulted the pickets by the
time Oldfield had hit the ground. But Adelaide is Australia's most
genteel city, and somehow England escaped. Maybe the police
presence deterred any would-be troublemakers, or maybe it was
the alarming way that Oldfield lay so still. The England players
hurried to his side, and were relieved to find him relatively intact.
'It's not your fault, Harold,' was his gentlemanly verdict, as he
was escorted groggily from the field. Despite a hairline fracture,

I predict a riot: England players surround Oldfield, his
skull fractured by a top-edged hook off Larwood; Woodfull,
in civvies, hurries to the stricken batsman. The crowd
bubbled with anger, but never quite boiled over

Oldfield would recover in time to play in the final Test, just over
a month later.

In between calls to the emergency services, a game of cricket
was going on. Set 532 on the fifth day, Australia dug in through a
partnership of contrasts: Woodfull blocking up one end; Bradman
leaping around like a leprechaun at the other. Their scores were
similar: 73 for Woodfull and 66 for Bradman, but Woodfull took
four times longer over his runs. Afterwards, he was said to favour
dropping Bradman from the side.

Fingleton also took a dim view of
Bradman's tactics. 'That innings . . . when
he moved feet to the off and then feet to
the leg before Larwood delivered the ball . . .
was all very thrilling if one did not stop to
think that this was a Test match, not village
green cricket, and that Australia was staging

**'To put the
matter bluntly he
was frightened of
fast bowling.'**

Warwick Armstrong
on Bradman

a burdensome uphill fight.' Warwick Armstrong, now a columnist on the *Evening News*, expressed a typically trenchant view: 'To put the matter bluntly he was frightened of fast bowling.'

Bradman did his best to refute such criticism, claiming that 'my method of playing Larwood exposed me to considerably more danger than the orthodox way'. But he was finding it hard, for once, to silence the critics. Larwood knew instinctively that he was winning the battle. 'As soon as Don started darting to and fro across the wicket I knew I had him worried,' he wrote in his autobiography. 'I used to say to myself as I bowled to Bradman: "I've got you frightened. Wait till I give you this one."'

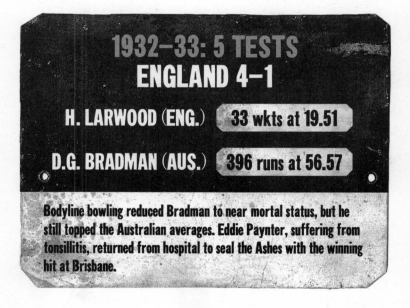

1932–33: 5 TESTS
ENGLAND 4–1

H. LARWOOD (ENG.) 33 wkts at 19.51

D.G. BRADMAN (AUS.) 396 runs at 56.57

Bodyline bowling reduced Bradman to near mortal status, but he still topped the Australian averages. Eddie Paynter, suffering from tonsillitis, returned from hospital to seal the Ashes with the winning hit at Brisbane.

THE CABLE WAR

While Woodfull performed his impersonation of a human shield, the Australian Board of Control (BOC) were preparing to open up a new front in the conflict. If their players could find no answer to Bodyline, perhaps they might challenge it through official channels. Bypassing Warner – who had played the innocent throughout – the BOC sent a cable direct to MCC.

This is their statement in full: 'Body-line bowling has assumed such proportions as to menace the best interest of the game, making protection of the body by the batsmen the main consideration. This is causing intensely bitter feeling between the players as well as injury. In our opinion it is unsportsmanlike. Unless stopped at once, it is likely to upset the friendly relations existing between Australia and England.'

Seventy years on, the BOC's cable reads sensibly and succinctly. But they made a grave mistake in using that dread word 'unsportsmanlike'. Unsporting? England? It was the most grievous slur in the dictionary. They might as well have accused Jardine of necrophilia.

MCC's legion of lawyers and diplomats creaked into action at once. The Lord's pavilion had not seen such activity in years. But rather than pinging a hostile response straight back at the BOC, they opted for the slower delivery, ruminating for five days over a suitably imperious reply. Their cable, when it eventually landed, struck a note of almost hysterical indignation. It was the same tone that the president of the golf club might use, after being caught with a lacy G-string in his blazer pocket.

'We, Marylebone Cricket Club, deplore your cable. We deprecate your opinion that there has been unsportsmanlike play.

'In our opinion it [Bodyline] is unsportsmanlike. Unless stopped at once, it is likely to upset the friendly relations existing between Australia and England.'

Australian Board of Control cable to MCC

We have fullest confidence in captain, team and managers and are convinced that they would do nothing to infringe either the laws of Cricket or the spirit of the game. We have no evidence that our confidence has been misplaced. Much as we regret accidents to Woodfull and Oldfield, we understand that in neither case was the bowler to blame. If the Australian Board of Control wish to propose a new Law or Rule, it shall receive our careful consideration in due course.

'We hope the situation is not now as serious as your cable would seem to indicate, but if it is such as to jeopardise the good relations between English and Australian cricketers and you consider it desirable to cancel the remainder of the programme we should consent, but with great reluctance.'

The final section was no more than a bluff. MCC knew that the BOC were cashing in on Bodyline. England's head-hunting operation made great box office, with attendance figures for the Melbourne Test breaking all known records. So when Jardine said he would not play another match until the accusation of poor sportsmanship was retracted, the BOC found themselves in a tight spot. Eventually, after some chivvying from the Australian government, they sent a placatory cable back to MCC: 'We do not regard the sportsmanship of your team as being in question . . . It is the particular class of bowling referred to therein which we consider is not in the best interest of cricket.'

With Jardine exonerated, the series could be concluded. To everyone's relief, the final two Tests failed to provoke the same levels of controversy. The first was played on a placid pitch at Brisbane, where Eddie Paynter famously returned from hospital in defiance of his tonsillitis to strike a decisive 83. The second featured the Test debut of H.H. 'Bull' Alexander, an Australian

> **'They said I was a "killer with the ball", without taking into account that Bradman, with the bat, was the greatest killer of all.'**
>
> Harold Larwood

fast bowler brought in to fight fire with fire. Though he scored one resounding hit on Jardine's ribs, Alexander took one wicket for 154 in the match and never played again.

The Bodyline storm had blown itself out. Jardine's England were the victors, by a healthy 4–1 margin, but at what cost? The bitterness of the affair had broken out of the narrow world of cricket and crossed over into the political sphere. At one point, it seemed as if it might scupper economic relations between England and Australia. As J.H. Thomas, the cabinet secretary for the Dominions, told an audience at Claridges: 'No politics ever introduced in the British Empire ever caused as much trouble as this damn Bodyline bowling.' Even US President Franklin D. Roosevelt had to be informed of this unlikely threat to geopolitical harmony, though he must have wondered whether he was the victim of some bizarre practical joke.

The final word should go to the Earl of Dartmouth, one of MCC's elder statesmen, who was moved to verse by the first BOC cable: 'We have fought / We have won / We have lost / But we have never squealed before.'

THE MOST HATED MAN IN AUSTRALIA

During an Ashes reunion lunch in the 1950s, Australian prime minister Robert Menzies gave a speech describing himself as 'the man in Australia whose parentage has been most often questioned'. Douglas Jardine, sitting at the back of the hall, raised a hand and interjected: 'Surely, sir, I still hold that honour.'

Heckle for heckle, Jardine must have attracted more barracking from the crowd than any other tourist to Australia, before or since. Even on his first visit, under Percy Chapman in 1928–29, he had to put up with lines like 'Eh, Mr Jardine, where's the butler to carry your bat for you?' There were also calls to 'Take that bloody hat off!' Jardine insisted on wearing a colourful Harlequin cap when batting, a symbol of his public-school background and amateur status. Hence the other popular line from that series: 'When are you going to get a move on, Rainbow?'

> **'They don't seem to like you very much over here, Mr Jardine.'**
> **'It's f***ing mutual.'**
> Exchange between England batsman 'Patsy' Hendren and his captain

Chapman, who had been to Cambridge, wore a 'jazz-hat' of his own. But Chapman could get away with it; he had the common touch. Fingleton described an incident at a rural railway station when England's three amateurs went for a

Jardine at Sydney, January 1933. Gubby Allen wrote in a letter home, 'Jardine is loathed . . . more than any German who fought in any war'

stroll along the platform: 'A stranger accosted them with a cheery greeting . . . Jardine's reply was a supercilious stare and complete ignorance of the proffered hand . . . Chapman and White warmly shook hands with the countryman.'

Jardine's 140 against New South Wales on that tour was arguably the finest and most daring innings of a largely constipated career. Bradman, who was shortly to make his Test debut, described it as one of the best exhibitions of strokeplay he had ever seen. But the punters were less impressed. The noise of their jeering all but drowned out the band. Finally dismissed, Jardine passed the incoming batsman, Patsy Hendren, on the way to the dressing-room. 'They don't seem to like you very much over here, Mr Jardine,' said Hendren. 'It's f***ing mutual,' came the heartfelt reply.

Jardine almost seemed to feed off the crowd's hatred. There have been modern players, Mike Atherton among them,

> **'A cricket tour in Australia would be the most delightful period in your life – if you were deaf.'**
> **Harold Larwood**

who liked to stoke themselves up by starting an argument with the close fielders. Perhaps Jardine was thinking along similar lines during the notorious Adelaide Test when he promoted himself to open the innings only minutes after Oldfield's horrific injury. 'Listen to the bastards yelling,' he said. 'I think I'll go in myself and give the bastards something to yell at.' Larwood wrote: 'I shall never forget Jardine in that moment . . . Jardine had cold courage. When he broke the shoulder of his bat and sent to the dressing-room for another one, he was advised from the mounds over and over again: "You won't need it, you bastard!"'

Jardine, whose sense of humour was surprisingly wry, had his own favourite pieces of barracking. Batting against 'Bull' Alexander in the final Test, he called for the twelfth man to bring him some water. A voice boomed from Sydney's famous Hill:

'Leave our flies alone, Jardine! They're the only flamin' friends you've got here!'

A barracker chides Jardine for swatting away a fly, 1932–33

'Don't give the bastard a drink – let him die of thirst.' Another wag noticed him trying to brush a fly away from his face and shouted out: 'Leave our flies alone, Jardine! They're the only flamin' friends you've got here!' But the best-remembered Bodyline wisecrack had nothing to do with the larrikins in the stands. According to legend, it came when Jardine knocked on Australia's dressing-room door to complain. He said he had overheard a fielder calling him a 'Pommy bastard'. Vic Richardson, Australia's combative vice-captain, looked around the room and drawled: 'All right, which one of you bastards called this bastard a bastard?'

A CATHOLIC CONSPIRACY?

Bodyline would have lost much of its bite if only Australia had possessed a few decent pacemen of their own. Instead, they opened the bowling with an old-fashioned seam/spin double-act: Thomas 'Tim' Wall from one end; Bill 'Tiger' O'Reilly from the other. The nicknames were misleading. Wall was the one striving for pace, though he turned out to be something of a sheep in wolf's clothing. O'Reilly, by contrast, was a feisty, John McEnroe type of character. He bowled medium-paced leg-breaks, top-spinners and googlies with the fury of a man stung by a bee.

O'Reilly finished as Australia's biggest success story of the series. While Larwood and Co. were collecting scalps, he kept piling up the wickets − 27 of them in all. Nobody noticed, of course. He might as well have been playing a penny whistle in the middle of a brass band. But O'Reilly was not easily discouraged. Bradman discovered this on their first meeting, in a country match between Wingello and Bowral when he was still 17.

The game was played on successive Saturdays, and at the halfway point Bradman was 234 not out. The match resumed on a beautiful day, as O'Reilly remembered it. 'The sun shone, the birds sang sweetly and the flowers bloomed as never before,' he wrote. 'I bowled him first ball with a leg-break which came from the leg stump to hit the off bail. Suddenly cricket was the best game in the whole wide world.'

Bradman and O'Reilly were boys from the sticks, near-neighbours in bush-town New South Wales. They were both completely untutored, and took a disparaging view of coaches. Bradman taught himself to bat by repetitively throwing a golf ball at a water-butt, then hitting it with a stump. O'Reilly and his three brothers chiselled a piece of Banksia tree-root into a rough sphere, and carved a bat out of a gum-tree. Robinson Crusoe would have approved.

One might have expected their shared background to bring them together. And they were certainly happy to eulogise each other *as cricketers*. Bradman went so far as to describe O'Reilly as the best bowler he ever faced. But as with Tony Blair and Gordon Brown, their mateship was reserved for camera lenses and reporters' notebooks. The division was based partly on temperament and partly on religion. Bradman was a Protestant, and – as we have seen – a dry character in every sense. He never smoked and didn't touch alcohol until later life, when he developed a scholarly interest in wine.

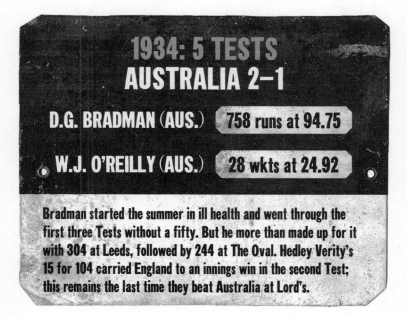

1934: 5 TESTS
AUSTRALIA 2–1

D.G. BRADMAN (AUS.)   758 runs at 94.75

W.J. O'REILLY (AUS.)   28 wkts at 24.92

Bradman started the summer in ill health and went through the first three Tests without a fifty. But he more than made up for it with 304 at Leeds, followed by 244 at The Oval. Hedley Verity's 15 for 104 carried England to an innings win in the second Test; this remains the last time they beat Australia at Lord's.

O'Reilly was of Irish Catholic stock, and like the other Irish Catholics in the side – Fingleton, McCabe, Leo O'Brien and 'Chuck' Fleetwood-Smith – he enjoyed a beer and a yarn in the bar at the end of play. As the 1930s wore on, the shamrock brigade formed an increasingly powerful clique. During the long steamship journeys to England, Bradman became ever more irritated by the pointed way in which they all trooped off to Mass together. After retirement, he would complain that Fingleton was the ring-leader, a man who 'conducted a vendetta against me all his life'.

'Fingleton conducted a vendetta against me all his life.'

Don Bradman

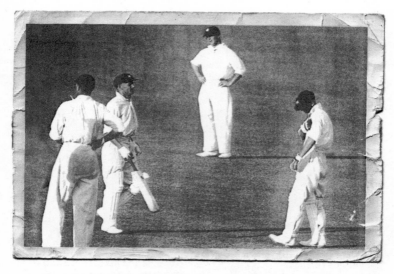

Stan McCabe rubs his chest after taking a blow at Brisbane: his 187 not out at Sydney was the innings of the 1932–33 series. 'He had qualities that even Bradman hadn't got,' remarked Len Hutton

CAPTAIN BRADMAN AND THE MUTINEERS

Having survived the Bodyline storm, Bradman nearly succumbed to appendicitis at the end of the 1934 tour. The infection was so bad that he could not sail home until the following year. Then, as the 1936–37 Ashes approached, he was appointed captain: the world's greatest cricketer was finally working for himself. The results, at first, were disappointing. England's seamers bowled Australia to defeat in the first two Tests. There was no secret weapon this time; just a glut of rain–affected pitches, which made the ball jump about like popcorn in a pan.

Throughout his career, Bradman never came to terms with the challenges of these 'sticky dogs'; indeed, his repeated failures on 'gluepots' constituted the one blot on his record. He refused to let nature dictate the way he should play, flashing the blade when he should have been dropping the anchor. As Fingleton wrote: 'He came in a hurry and invariably left in a hurry, as if he were in the middle of a telephone conversation in the pavilion . . . and had asked the caller to hold the line.'

The third Test also featured heavy rain, but this time Bradman had devised a way of annoying all his opponents – both inside the

'Bradman was the Efficient Age which followed the Golden Age. Victor Trumper was the Flying Bird; Bradman the aeroplane.'

Neville Cardus

tent and out. With the pitch drying out on the second evening, he reversed the batting order and sent in his old friends, O'Reilly and Fleetwood-Smith. 'Why me?' asked Fleetwood-Smith. Bradman replied: 'Chuck, you can't get out unless you hit the ball. Now, you can't hit the ball on a good wicket, so you've got no chance of hitting it out there.' As Bradman admitted years later, Fleetwood-Smith 'didn't relish the remark too much'. Still, there was some logic to it: he got through the last overs of the day without the ball hitting either his bat or his stumps.

When Bradman did finally go in, at 97 for five, England tried out a dastardly scheme of their own. The idea was that Bill Voce would start with a short one, and that Walter Robins would backpedal from square-leg to deep-square as the ball was bowled. It worked a treat, in that Bradman hooked in the air, straight to Robins – who dropped the catch. At the next change of over, Robins muttered an apology to his captain, Gubby Allen, who let it hang in the air for a second. Then he replied, with pained irony: 'Oh, don't give it another thought. You've just cost us the Ashes, that's all.'

Australia did indeed wind up easy winners, courtesy of Bradman's 270. But as the team prepared to celebrate a tide-turning victory, the Board of Control sprung another surprise. They summoned four players they believed were giving Bradman trouble – O'Reilly, Fleetwood-Smith, McCabe and O'Brien – and read them a long, vague statement. There were coded accusations of insubordination, poor fitness, late hours and heavy drinking. But it was never made clear who was the source, or who the target.

Eventually O'Reilly lost his patience and burst out: 'What's this, a game of tiggy-touch, is it?' The meeting had the effect of enraging both sides of the dressing-room, as Bradman had been

Bill O'Reilly: '. . . proof that spin bowling was not necessarily a gentle art,' said his 1992 *Wisden* obituary. Bradman considered him the greatest bowler he ever faced

D.G. BRADMAN (AUS.) 810 runs at 90.00

W.J. O'REILLY (AUS.) 25 wkts at 22.20

England took an unexpected 2–0 lead, dismissing Australia for 58 and 80 in successive innings at Brisbane and Sydney. But this only spurred Bradman to yet another unique feat: he is still the only captain in history to win a Test series after going 2–0 down.

neither consulted nor informed about the board's plans. When the suits explained to him that 'We wanted you to be completely innocent and at arm's length so that you knew nothing about it,' Bradman replied: 'You can't possibly expect them to believe that.'

In 1988, Bradman told a radio interviewer that: 'the players . . . recognised that I'd been placed in an embarrassing position and it wasn't my fault'. But O'Reilly wasn't so sure. 'I never really forgave him for it,' he said. 'I still haven't forgiven him now.'

A FEUD RENEWED

The 1930s were a time of global depression, especially where Wally Hammond was concerned. It was bad enough being outscored by Bradman, but by the second half of the decade he was being outranked as well. So Hammond came up with a cunning plan. If he took a day job, sacrificed his match fees and became an amateur, he would become a contender for the England captaincy. Then, perhaps, he could meet Bradman on equal terms again.

Hammond had long been pally with Pelham Warner, whose reward for a pusillanimous performance as Jardine's tour manager was to be appointed England's chairman of selectors. So when Hammond's new role as a director of Marsham's Tyres was announced, in November 1937, everyone understood the subtext: he would be leading England in the following year's Ashes.

> **'Basil, that Wally Hammond of yours really is a wonderful chap, isn't he?' 'If you want my honest opinion, I think he's an absolute shit.'**
> **Exchange between 'Plum' Warner and Basil Allen**

The move was not universally popular. Over pink gins at Lord's, MCC members could be heard muttering that they would rather have seen communists running the country than a car salesman captaining England.

And then there was Basil Allen, Hammond's predecessor as Gloucestershire captain. On one occasion during a Gentlemen v Players match, Warner turned to Allen and gushed: 'Basil, that Wally Hammond of yours really is a wonderful chap, isn't he?' 'If you want my honest opinion,' Allen replied, 'I think he's an absolute shit.'

The calm before the run-fest: a dapper-looking Don Bradman and Wally Hammond toss at The Oval, 1938. Groundsman 'Bosser' Martin looks on

The appointment was not an immediate success. Though Hammond made 240 in the second Test of 1938, Bradman more than matched him with hundreds in each of the first three games. Australia reached the final Test at The Oval with a 1–0 lead and the Ashes secured. But Hammond did have the last laugh, even if it was a hollow and humourless one. Winning the toss, on a pitch so docile it could have put New York to sleep, he told his team: 'No score is too high.' They didn't let him down: Len Hutton made 364 out of 903 for seven declared. Bradman never even had a chance to bat, as he broke an ankle bone during a rare visit to the bowling crease.

When England had completed their victory – by the record margin of an innings and 579 runs – O'Reilly demanded: 'Where's the groundsman's hut? If I had a rifle, I'd shoot him now.' He might have used a different figure of speech if he had

'In all this Australian team, there are barely one or two who would be accepted as public school men.'

C.B. Fry on the 1938 Australians

known what was coming. On 3 September 1939, a green baize was placed over the Long Room busts at Lord's, prompting one MCC member to exclaim: 'Did you see that, sir? That means war!'

Bradman enlisted at once with the Royal Australian Air Force, but was soon discharged for medical reasons. Not only was he suffering from a bad back, but the same laser-powered eyes that had transfixed so many bowlers were somehow found to be defective. Hammond also took a position in the flying corps, in which he enjoyed a thoroughly cushy war: some welfare work, a few exhibition matches, and several visits to South Africa. This might seem an odd place for an RAF officer to be frequenting, until you realise that it was the home of his favourite mistress (and future second wife), Durban beauty queen Sybil Ness-Harvey.

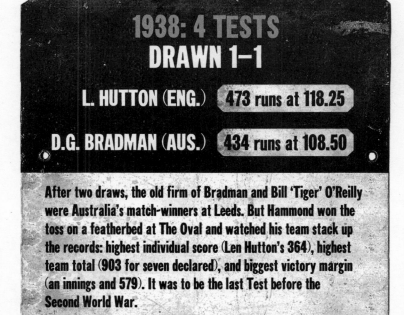

1938: 4 TESTS
DRAWN 1–1

L. HUTTON (ENG.) 473 runs at 118.25

D.G. BRADMAN (AUS.) 434 runs at 108.50

After two draws, the old firm of Bradman and Bill 'Tiger' O'Reilly were Australia's match-winners at Leeds. But Hammond won the toss on a featherbed at The Oval and watched his team stack up the records: highest individual score (Len Hutton's 364), highest team total (903 for seven declared), and biggest victory margin (an innings and 579). It was to be the last Test before the Second World War.

THE IKIN CATCH

When the Ashes resumed in 1946–47, both Bradman and Hammond were reappointed as captain. This would have been the perfect moment for a personal ceasefire. Hammond had been a model of chivalry during the 1945 'Victory Tests', which pitted England against a united Australian services team. When the visitors suffered an injury to their wicketkeeper, he even popped round to the services' dressing-room to suggest they use a twelfth man.

Such sporting gestures were soon forgotten in the heat of the 1946-47 Ashes. The contest burst into flame on the very first morning. Australia had lost two wickets and Bradman was batting erratically when he edged a ball from Bill Voce to Jack Ikin at second slip. There was a strange moment as the players all stood

stock-still, as if someone upstairs had pressed the pause button. Eventually Ikin seemed to realise that Bradman was not going to walk, and appealed. But the umpire, George Borwick, shook his head.

Hammond was furious, and as he walked past the batsman and umpire at the end of the over he muttered:

An ageing Wally Hammond enjoys a cuppa and a smoke, August 1946

'A fine bloody way to start a series.'

Hammond to Bradman as 'the Don' declines to walk

'A fine bloody way to start a series.' The furore was such that Bradman was forced into making a rare statement to the press. He explained that he thought the ball might have bounced on its way to Ikin, and as he could not be sure that it hadn't, he had stood his ground and waited for the umpire's decision.

No one else was in much doubt. The consensus was that the ball had taken the top edge of the bat as Bradman tried to cut it away behind square. Up in the Australian dressing-room, Keith Miller had grabbed his gloves and was already preparing to walk out to the crease. The incident might have been quickly forgotten, were it not for what came next. Bradman seemed invigorated when he returned for the afternoon session. A little bad blood had gone down wonderfully well with lunch, and he promptly forged on to 187 out of Australia's 645 all out. Now the heavens opened, in one of Brisbane's spectacular hailstorms. For Hammond, it was the final insult. Had Bradman gone for 28, England would already have been working their way to a match-winning lead. Instead, they were looking at an impossible rearguard on a venomous pitch.

The question is, did Bradman know the catch was a good one? He had every motivation to bend the rules. His health and form were poor enough to provoke widespread speculation that he might soon retire. And then there was the ongoing feud with Hammond. When his team-mates noticed him chuckling during that fateful hailstorm, he explained: 'In my last pre-war Test England scored more than 900 before Hammond declared and I couldn't bat because I'd broken my ankle bowling. Now things have swung the other way, do you blame me for being happy?'

But Fingleton, who had every reason to find Bradman guilty, ended up taking the opposite view. He argued that while Bradman had many faults, bad sportsmanship had never been among them. 'At this time in Brisbane he was playing poor cricket, possibly the poorest of his Test career,' Fingleton wrote. 'His mind was troubled and probably he did not realise that he had given a catch.'

The real loser in this whole saga was not cricket, as some romantics would have it, but Hammond himself. At 43, his body was creaking even more than Bradman's, and this latest disappointment seemed to finish him off. On the field, he failed to contribute a single half-century; off it, he insisted on travelling separately from the team, in a Jaguar supplied by some private admirer.

Denis Compton, England's leading run-scorer on the tour, was desperate to have dinner with Hammond and 'soak up the aura of the great man'. Instead, he was shocked to find Australia's captain more welcoming and receptive than his own. He wrote: 'Of the several tours I have made . . . it was the worst example of mismanagement from the top I encountered. The players looked to the captain for guidance and it was not there. The only time we saw him was at the grounds.'

MILLER AND LINDWALL: AUSSIES IN EXCELSIS

Such was Australia's fast-bowling vacuum through the 1930s that England's Bodyliners must have thought they had got away with murder. And with the exception of one or two post-war veterans, they were right. Payback did eventually arrive, but not until 1946-47, when Ray Lindwall and Keith Miller finally provided Bradman with a strike force worthy of the name.

> **'Pressure is a Messerschmitt up your arse. Playing cricket is not.'**
>
> Keith Miller

Perhaps it was poetic justice that the young Lindwall had spent that troubled summer of 1932–33 imitating Harold Larwood's perfectly calibrated action. By the time the Ashes resumed, Lindwall had mastered the mechanics of the art, honing his delivery stride to the nearest millimetre. A new generation of schoolboys copied his style, while a generation of batsmen cowered from his skidding bouncer.

'Nugget' Miller had a simpler method: an apparently innocuous saunter to the wicket, a violent heave of the shoulder, and – more often than not – a hostile, lifting 'jaffa' for the batsman to contend with. He could bat, too, with a devil-may-care flourish

and a total disregard for bowlers' reputations. A Mosquito fighter
pilot during the war, he used to scoff at the sensitivities of modern
sportsmen. 'I'll tell you what pressure is,' he would say. 'Pressure
is a Messerschmitt up your arse. Playing cricket is not.'

Miller embodied the ideal of Aussie manhood. He was
bronzed and clean-limbed, if not necessarily clean-living. He
shared advertising duties for Brylcreem's hair products with
England's Denis Compton, another charismatic young star. But
while Compton had the sheen of a matinée idol, Miller was
earthier. He bridged the gap between everyman and superman.

Bradman found Miller's lifestyle rather too catholic – with a small 'C' this time – for his taste. Miller would arrive back at the hotel in a tuxedo while Bradman was coming down for breakfast, then refuse to bowl later in the day because he had a sore back. When Bradman finally retired, and started running Australian cricket instead of defining it, he did his best to make sure that this wastrel was never given a crack at the captaincy.

It is true that Miller could be lackadaisical at times during his state captaincy career. In one match he accidentally took the field with 12 players, then barked: 'One of you bugger off and the rest scatter.' But he was a natural leader of men, and won many more games than he lost. Bradman's snub only threw him back into his whirl of cocktails and conquests with renewed vigour.

The story goes that, at one point during the 1956 Ashes tour, Miller was feeling worn out after a particularly heavy week. But just as he was hanging up the 'Do Not Disturb' sign, there was a knock on the door. Lord Mountbatten, aptly described as

'One of you bugger off and the rest scatter.'

Keith Miller sets his field

the team's liaison manager, told him a young woman wanted to meet him. 'I don't care if it's the Queen of England,' Miller said, 'I'm having a night in.' Mountbatten replied: 'It's not the Queen of England, but it is her sister Margaret.' *Noblesse oblige*, as they say, and Miller's quiet night had to be put on hold.

THE MORALITY OF BOUNCERS

Miller could have been born to play Test cricket. But when he finally made his debut, at Brisbane in November 1946, he was less than enchanted by what he found. With the ball turning somersaults on a drying pitch, he wanted to drop his pace to avoid causing someone an injury. But the ruthless Bradman insisted that he show no mercy.

'I remember hitting Bill Edrich and Wally Hammond,' Miller remembered, in a revealing 1970s interview. 'Edrich, a chunky, gutsy little chap with a Distinguished Flying Cross was getting battered from pillar to bloody post . . . Bradman came over to me and said: "Bowl faster, bowl faster. Get them out." He told me later, when you play Test cricket you don't give these Englishmen an inch, play it tough, flat out the whole way. "Grind them into the dust" were his words.

'I thought to myself that a war had just gone and a lot of Test cricketers and future Test cricketers had been killed . . . So I thought: "Bugger me. If that's Test cricket then they can stick it up their . . ." Don kept up this incessant will-to-win which just wasn't my way of playing cricket.'

'Grind them into the dust.'

Bradman advises Keith Miller on how to tackle the Poms

This might seem a bit ironic, coming from Miller – a hot-tempered bowler who was soon accumulating a long rap-sheet for intimidation and battery. When Godfrey Evans spent 97 minutes on nought at Adelaide, it was Miller who bowled him two successive bouncers, then remarked: 'Sorry

Ray Lindwall, Miller's co-pilot during Australia's demolition
of England in 1948. 'Poetry!' said a smitten 'Plum' Warner
of Lindwall's classical fast bowling

Godfrey, but I have to do it – the
crowd are a bit bored at the moment.'

The following year at Trent Bridge,
he enraged the crowd by bouncing Len
Hutton five times in eight balls. *Wisden*'s
account of that 1948 tour suggested that
Miller's 'habit of wheeling round, flying
into an abnormally fast start and tossing
back his head before releasing the ball
gave an impression that petulance more
than cricket tactics dictated his methods at such times'.

> **'Sorry Godfrey, but I have to do it – the crowd are a bit bored at the moment.'**
>
> Keith Miller bounces a slow-scoring Godfrey Evans

Yet despite the occasional blow-out, Miller and Lindwall
did have scruples about the way they bowled. True, they were
more than ready to test out recognised batsmen with the bouncer,
particularly if there was a suspicion of windiness. (As Lindwall
put it: 'There is no sitting duck like a scared duck.') But against
tailenders, or on particularly spiteful pitches, they preferred to keep
their most dangerous weapons sheathed. The fast bowler's code of
omertà was demonstrated in a New South Wales match when the

'You've just insulted all fast bowlers. You've admitted that No. 8 can bat better than you can bowl.'

Ray Lindwall chides Alan Davidson for bouncing a lower-order batsman

left-armer Alan Davidson bounced the opposition No. 8. 'You've just insulted all fast bowlers,' Lindwall scolded him. 'You've admitted that No. 8 can bat better than you can bowl.'

While Miller was equally considerate towards tailenders, he never flinched from roughing up his drinking buddies. In fact, he positively revelled in it. The England fast bowler Frank Tyson wrote: 'If there was no Compton in the opposition he derived little enjoyment from bowling bouncers.'

There was a memorable passage of play at Melbourne in 1954–55 when Miller, now 35, roused himself to take three wickets in seven overs. After beating Compton's outside edge with one lifting leg-cutter, he turned to the non-striker Colin Cowdrey and said: 'It's amazing, young Colin. They keep picking this joker, Compton – I suppose for his looks – but I've been bowling him this same ball since 1946 and he still doesn't wake up to it!'

BRADMAN'S LAST STAND

Of all the summers to be an England batsman, 1948 was probably the most torrid. It wasn't just the fury of Miller and Lindwall, or the hours spent chasing leather in the field. The real killer was a masochistic new regulation that allowed a new ball every 55 overs. This was a fast bowler's charter. In some of their innings, England's total had barely reached three figures before Australia's quicks returned for a second burst, armed with a new red cherry. Batting must have felt like swimming in heavy seas – every time you put a few strokes together, another ten-foot wave rolled in to slap you back again.

'The Don was too good: he spoilt the game.'
England's Jack Hobbs on Bradman, 1952

But there was one batsman who welcomed the new rule. On his last tour, Bradman's burning ambition was to go round the country unbeaten. And with a third speedster in his armoury – the burly left-armer Bill Johnston – he must have chuckled at this MCC own goal. His three-pronged pace trident ended up spearing 67 wickets, four more than Australia lost in the whole series.

England's batsmen were scattered like tommies under machine-gun fire, and her generals panicked. After the second Test, Len Hutton was dropped for the heinous crime of backing away from the ball (an accusation that was easy to make from the safety of the committee room). E.W. Swanton, *Daily Telegraph* cricket writer and establishment propagandist, later justified the move on the grounds that 'I never saw Len flinch again for the rest of his career.'

Compton, though, was full of the Dunkirk spirit. At Trent Bridge he held out for almost seven hours, scoring 184 before Miller's umpteenth bouncer forced him back onto his stumps. Then, at Old Trafford, he took a blow from Lindwall, who encroached well onto the pitch before releasing a vicious no-ball. Compton went to hook, but only succeeded in top-edging the ball into his own forehead – *à la* Bert Oldfield at Adelaide (see page 109).

In his autobiography, Lindwall claimed that Compton had said: 'It's not your fault, Ray.' He also had the cheek to blame the injury on Compton's late decision to change his shot, after hearing the call of 'no-ball'. The fact that he had let the ball go from something like 20 yards was conveniently forgotten. Compton left a trail of blood as he tottered back to the dressing-room. Three hours later – after a few stitches, two slugs of brandy,

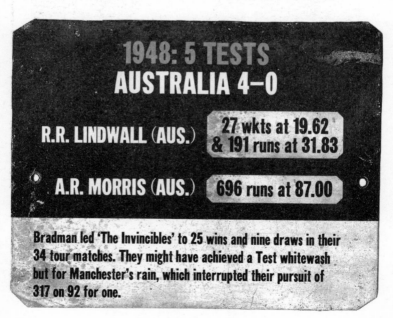

1948: 5 TESTS
AUSTRALIA 4–0

R.R. LINDWALL (AUS.) — 27 wkts at 19.62 & 191 runs at 31.83

A.R. MORRIS (AUS.) — 696 runs at 87.00

Bradman led 'The Invincibles' to 25 wins and nine draws in their 34 tour matches. They might have achieved a Test whitewash but for Manchester's rain, which interrupted their pursuit of 317 on 92 for one.

Skulled: Denis Compton cops a short one from Lindwall at
Old Trafford. After a stiff brandy, Compton returned to blast
a fearless 145 and breathe boozy fumes over the close fielders

> **'That bugger Bradman never had a tear in his eye throughout his whole life.'**
>

and a quick net to see if he could still see the ball – he returned to strike an undefeated 145. 'Great as Compton is, never has he been greater,' intoned Leslie Mitchell over the famous *Movietone News* footage.

Compton's resistance, plus a day of rain, earned England their only draw of the series. But while Bradman may not have equalled Warwick Armstrong's 1921 whitewash, his team achieved something even more remarkable: an undefeated record through all 34 first-class matches. The 1948 'Invincibles' have gone down

'For he's a jolly good batsman': England's fielders applaud Bradman, in his last Test innings, and pray that he doesn't change his mind

> **' . . . in a lot of ways Bradman did a tremendous amount of damage to Australian cricket. He didn't ever come clean as a personal member of the side, he was always a far distant relative.'**
>
> Bill O'Reilly

as the finest bunch of cricketers ever to dock at Tilbury.

Bradman claimed to be unaware that when he walked out to bat in the final Test, he needed just four runs to average 100 in Test cricket. He never got them. The master batsman propped forward to his second ball, from Warwickshire's unheralded leg-spinner Eric Hollies, and was bowled by a well-disguised googly.

There is a marvellous poignancy in the fact that Bradman, the great automaton, turned out to be flesh and blood in the end. And perhaps it says something about the human condition that sport's most dominant individual is remembered as much for his failures as his triumphs. The Australian Broadcasting Corporation took their PO Box number – 9994 – from his final average (minus the decimal point).

'It's not easy to bat with tears in your eyes,' said Bradman afterwards. But England's close fielders were not convinced. 'Get away with you,' was the view of Jack Crapp at first slip. 'That bugger Bradman never had a tear in his eye throughout his whole life.'

IN SEARCH OF BRIGHTER CRICKET

1950–1970

LORD HAWKE'S PRAYER REJECTED

Bradman's retirement, like everything else he did, had a polarising effect. Players on both sides suddenly found themselves breathing easier, as if there was more oxygen in the room. For the bean-counters, though, this was a period of mourning. Attendance figures in 1950–51 were down on the previous series by more than a quarter.

No one could accuse the 1950–51 Ashes of being dull. The series revolved, quite literally, around the middle finger of Jack Iverson – an outlandish mystery spinner who flicked the ball out like a man making a rude gesture. Known to his team-mates as 'Freak', Iverson developed this revolutionary technique with a ping-pong ball, while playing French cricket on army service in New Guinea. He was 35 when he finally broke into the Australian team – an old man in a hurry. After taking 21 wickets in those five Tests, he melted away as suddenly as he had appeared.

It was a disappointing series for England – who lost 4-1 under the gallant leadership of Freddie Brown – but an excellent one for barracking. When Eric Hollies' leg-spin was underused at the Sydney Cricket Ground, the cry went up: 'What's the matter – don't they bury their dead in Birmingham?' Hollies won the larrikins over with his quick-smart reply: 'No, they stuff 'em and send 'em out to Australia!'

Then there was John Warr, a medium-pacer who fell a notch or two short of Test standard. As England's ship docked in Sydney, one of the wharf labourers shouted: 'Hey Warr, you've got as much chance of taking a Test wicket on this tour as I have of

pushing a pound of butter up a parrot's arse with a hot needle.'

The wharfie was not far wrong. Warr bowled 73 eight-ball overs in his two Tests, conceding 281 runs and taking one solitary wicket. Even that one was a consolation prize. Ian Johnson gave himself out for a thin edge at Adelaide, in defiance of the umpire's shake of the head. 'Well, I saw John's shoulders sag,' Johnson explained, 'and he looked so crestfallen that on the spur of the moment I nodded to the umpire and walked.'

Ian Johnson's sportsmanship was in keeping with the overall atmosphere. At the end of the 1950–51 series, Keith Miller put his name to a newspaper article entitled: 'Test Cricket's Becoming Friendlier'. But good fellowship did not necessarily mean good

'What's the matter – don't they bury their dead in Birmingham?' 'No, they stuff 'em and send 'em out to Australia!'

Exchange between the Australian crowd
and England's underused leg-spinner Eric Hollies

> **'Hey Warr, you've got as much chance of taking a Test wicket on this tour as I have of pushing a pound of butter up a parrot's arse with a hot needle.'**
> An Australian barracker greets the England bowler John Warr

'I saw Len Hutton in his prime / Another time / another time.' *Poem* by Harold Pinter, 1986

1950–51: 5 TESTS
AUSTRALIA 4–1

J.B. IVERSON (AUS.) — 21 wkts at 15.24

L. HUTTON (ENG.) — 533 runs at 88.83

The first Test (Aus. 228 and 32–7 dec; Eng. 68–7 dec and 122) was described as the craziest ever played. Thunderstorms produced a classic Brisbane 'sticky dog' and a frenzy of declaration and counter-declaration. After that, Iverson's mystery spin kept a young England side off balance.

box office. For many Australians, the Ashes were not the Ashes without Don Bradman (or Sir Don Bradman, as he became in 1949). The fans missed their knight in white flannels, and his special talent for winding up the Poms.

Dwindling audiences around the globe prompted Norman Preston, editor of *Wisden*, to write in the 1952 *Almanack*: 'Cricket, and not just English cricket, needs an injection of culture and enterprise.' The cause was taken up by administrators in both countries under the slogan 'Brighter Cricket'. But the players took precious little notice. Throughout the 1950s and 60s, Ashes cricket was more attritional than aspirational.

Turning up for the first morning of the 1953 series, the Australians noted a disappointing absence of skydivers and dancing girls. There was one futuristic touch, however. After

> **'Remember lad, one day we'll have a fast bowler – and I hope that day isn't too far off.'**
>
> Len Hutton to Ray Lindwall after facing some torrid overs, 1950–51

two decades of Ashes frustration, the selectors had bowed to the inevitable and appointed Len Hutton captain. Lord Hawke's appeal to the supreme umpire – 'Pray God, no professional shall captain England' (see page 78) – had finally been turned down.

The top job took a bit of getting used to, especially as Hutton remained part of the rank and file at Yorkshire. Confusion arose when the selectors needed a spinner for the Lord's Test, and recalled the 1950–51 captain Freddie Brown. The two men had been friends and allies since that tour, but Hutton was damned if he could work out how to address his former boss.

Lindwall wrote: 'Throughout the match such gems of dialogue could be heard as "Would you like to take a turn at the top end, Skipper?" and "Well bowled, Skipper, have a break now would you?" The rest of the team followed Hutton's example with the strange result that they called the captain "Len" and one of their team-mates "Skipper".'

Hutton's new world was not exactly brave. He had two basic priorities: (a) that his batsmen should value their wickets, and (b) that his fast bowlers should husband their energies. The upshot was that England became much harder to beat, but the team's over-rate and scoring-rate fell through the floor.

This may not have been 'Brighter Cricket', but it was thoroughly in character. Hutton was the kind of opener who thought it too risky to essay a cut-shot before lunch. The epitome of the dour Yorkshireman, he brought a gritty pragmatism to the job. It was no coincidence that he also reclaimed the Ashes for the first time in two decades.

THE BLOCKER
AND THE CHUCKER

If Hutton was determined to wear the buggers
down, he found the perfect instrument in Trevor
Bailey, an Essex all-rounder who took a perverse
pride in his nickname: 'The Barnacle'. Bailey
once said: 'Cricket is a situation game. When the
situation is dead, the game is dead.' And no one
was better at killing it.

Time after time during that 1953 series, the Australians thought
they had England cornered. But Bailey was like a cartoon pest,
emerging from manhole covers and stepping out from behind
telegraph poles to thwart their ambitions. In the Lord's Test, when
he and Willie Watson held out for almost four hours to save the
match, E.W. Swanton wrote: 'I cannot remember when a crowd
so revelled in defence for defence's sake.'

Bailey had an almost morbid horror of defeat. The concept
of the gambit was quite alien to him. During that Lord's match,
England finished only 61 runs short of victory, with three wickets
still standing. Yet a gentle suggestion from Watson that England
should go for the runs met with a brusque response: 'Trevor just
turned his back on me and walked away.'

In classical terms, Bailey was a Stoic rather than a Corinthian.
In the Leeds Test he halted Australia's progress again, this time by
bowling yards down the leg-side as they chased 177 in the final
two hours. (Some 40 years later, similar tactics from Zimbabwe's
bowlers at Bulawayo would provoke England coach David Lloyd
into his infamous 'We flippin' murdered them' outburst. The
result was actually a draw with scores level.)

When the two sides gathered for the traditional post-match drink, the atmosphere was frosty. 'The Australians, every single one of them, were absolutely livid and I think rightly so,' wrote Godfrey Evans. 'They had been cheated of victory, they said, by the worst kind of negative cricket. They were right.'

The 1953 series started just nine days after the coronation of Queen Elizabeth II and the conquest of Everest. Yet the first four Tests failed to reflect the festive mood: after all this grim resistance, the teams were still locked at 0–0. On the morning of the final match, at The Oval, Fingleton wrote that: 'This appears to be a serious day for England – the last time I saw looks like this on the gentry in London was in the middle of the 1938 crisis.'

'Bailey, I wish you were a statue and I was a pigeon.'

Trevor Bailey fields another brickbat from Sydney's notorious Hill

England went in with three seamers: Alec Bedser, the steady-as-she-goes medium-pacer; Fred Trueman, a shock-haired Yorkshireman making his Ashes debut; and Bailey. But their biggest hope was invested in the spin duo of Jim Laker and Tony Lock. The Australians, by contrast, had put all their faith in pace. The captain, Lindsay Hassett, realised he had erred when Bedser's first ball took a bite out of the dry, powdery surface. He turned to Evans and remarked: 'I can see who this wicket's been made for.'

England's eight-wicket win was secured by Lock, a balding, bullying left-armer from the Bill O'Reilly mould. Lock had started out as an orthodox, toss-it-up sort of spinner, but over a winter spent training in a low-roofed indoor school in Croydon, he had started bending his arm to avoid scraping his knuckles. Now his trademark was the quicker yorker, bowled – or at least delivered – with a perceptible kink in the elbow. After losing his stumps to one Lock special, Essex's Doug Insole turned to the square-leg umpire and glowered: 'How was I out then – run out?'

The Australians were equally unimpressed. As Harvey put it: 'We all reckoned he threw his express delivery.' As far as they were concerned, Lock's five wickets brought a shabby conclusion to a shoddy series. Standing on The Oval balcony, Hassett looked

1953: 5 TESTS
ENGLAND 1–0

A.V. BEDSER (ENG.) | 39 wkts at 17.49

L. HUTTON (ENG.) | 443 runs at 55.38

Rain and Trevor Bailey kept Australia at bay until The Oval, where they were Laker-and-Locked. Hutton's patient (not to say tedious) captaincy carried England to their first series win since Bodyline.

out over a packed outfield and delivered the double-edged quip: 'England deserved to win, if not from the first ball at least from the second-last over.' Thousands of fans laughed uproariously, delighted at the urn's return for the first time since 1934.

England's former captain Walter Robins complimented Hassett on his wit, saying 'Well done Lindsay, that was absolutely perfect.' Hassett replied: 'Not bad, considering that Tony Lock chucked half our team out.'

THE TYPHOON BLOWS IN

'Noo, we 'aven't got much boolin',' Hutton teased reporters when he arrived in Australia for the 1954–55 series. 'Got a chap called Tyson but you won't 'ave 'eard of 'im because 'e's 'ardly ever played.'

Frank Tyson was indeed a virtual unknown, a 24-year-old fast man with less than a full season of county cricket behind him. His fresh face, when combined with rounded shoulders and wispy, receding hair, gave him the look of a middle-aged baby. But he was no soft touch: he had won his place on the tour by breaking Bill Edrich's jaw at Lord's with a brutal bouncer. Up in the Middlesex dressing-room, the watching Compton remarked: 'Just think how fast he will be at Sydney!' He then turned to Peter DeLisle, a quivering amateur, and said: 'I'm not ready. You'll have to go in.'

Tyson was certainly quick, so quick that Richie Benaud described him as 'the fastest I ever saw, fractionally shading Jeff Thomson'. But when his rhythm deserted him – as it did at Brisbane, in the first Test of 1954–55 – he could be innocuous. The Queensland climate was ill-suited to his 17-stride run-up; by the time he arrived at the crease, he was drenched in half a kilo of his own sweat. He took one for 160, letting the ball go with all the speed and menace of a pensioner playing *pétanque*.

The turning-point of Tyson's tour was a conversation with Alf Gover, the *Sunday Mirror*'s correspondent. Journalists are better

> **'. . . my headache had almost gone and my pride was ringing from the previous day's blow. I threw every effort into my bowling.'**
>
> **'Typhoon' Tyson returns after head-butting Lindwall's bouncer**

known for putting players down than putting them right, but Gover – a bowling coach and former England seamer – was a special case. He recommended that Tyson should shorten his run, and at that point something clicked. The ball stopped dying in the pitch and started flying around as if it was made of rubber.

In the first innings at Sydney, Ron Archer was caught at second slip off the face of his bat. He recalled: 'The ball was so fast that the force of it turned the bat in my hand. I can remember being able to watch the ball flying to Hutton at slip: he was so far back it was like being caught in the outfield.' Tyson's follow-up was to bounce Ray Lindwall, whom he felt had forfeited the tailender's traditional immunity by scoring 60 at Brisbane. It proved to be a fateful decision. First, Lindwall edged the ball and was caught behind. Then, when England's turn came to bat, Lindwall retaliated with a bouncer of his own, which struck the retreating Tyson on the back of the head and knocked him senseless. The bump could reportedly be seen from 100 yards away. As Tyson was stretchered off, Lindwall remarked to his Australian team-mates: 'I shouldn't have done that.' He was right. According to Hutton, 'When [Tyson] came out of his concussed state,

'I shouldn't have done that,' remarked Lindwall, after felling Frank Tyson with a bouncer. Australia went on to reap the whirlwind – or rather the Typhoon

I swear there was a new light in his eyes, as if a spark had been kindled deep down inside him . . . When he resumed bowling the next day he was a yard, maybe a yard and a half quicker than before.' Tyson finished with six wickets as Australia fell short by 38.

England were ecstatic. 'If we can get Ray to nut Frank again, there'll be no holding him,' they laughed. But in fact there was no need for a repeat prescription. Tyson had found his rhythm; for the rest of the series, he was unstoppable.

Tyson's heyday, like that of his boxing namesake, was as short as it was spectacular. He had little to offer apart from his raw speed, which began to tail off after a couple of seasons on Northamptonshire's sluggish pitches. But in the winter of 1954–55, the man they called 'The Typhoon' possessed a genuinely elemental force. On the eve of England's game against the Prime Minister's XI in Canberra, Lindsay Hassett was telling his former team-mates: 'I can't see that this fella Tyson's as fast as you all seem to think. When he bounces one at me, I'll hook him out of sight.' Just at that moment, there was a flash of lightning and a huge clap of thunder. 'There you are!' Hassett continued triumphantly. 'The Typhoon's started his run-up already.'

> **'I can't see that this fella Tyson's as fast as you all seem to think. When he bounces one at me, I'll hook him out of sight.'**
> **Lindsay Hassett underestimates 'Typhoon' Tyson, 1954–55**

LAKER SUPERIOR

After a few years of courteous co-existence, the 1956 series produced the biggest bust-up since Bodyline. Cricket lovers may now remember it as Jim Laker's great summer, but that was only half the story. England's blatant pitch-tampering poured a dose of napalm on previously tranquil waters.

It was Keith Miller who unknowingly set events in motion when his ten wickets won the Lord's Test. This could have been a crushing blow for Peter May, England's eager boy scout of a captain. But somewhere deep inside the pavilions of power, tough decisions were being taken. After the match, May warned the flagging Tyson: 'We won't be wanting you from here on, Frank. From now on, they [the pitches] will all be spinners.'

England's insistence on turning tracks was coloured as much by the weakness of Australia's spinners (Ian Johnson and Richie Benaud) as the strength of their own (Laker and Lock). The tactic was either canny or devious, depending whose side you were on. There is nothing in the Laws to dictate how a pitch is prepared, but every cricketer knows that too much grass favours the quicks and too little the slows. Some of those served up in 1956 could have been cut from King Lear's blasted heath.

'England cheated . . . ' fumed Australian opener Colin McDonald, before adding the rider: ' . . . if by cheating you include the practice of preparing wickets to suit your own purpose.'

May's purpose was the destruction of Australia's batting line-up, and his star turn was a tall Yorkshireman named Laker. There was a huge contrast between England's two principal spinners: where Lock bustled and ranted, Laker floated about in a lofty reverie, sometimes seeming to take little notice of the game going on around him.

Geoffrey Howard, manager of the Tyson tour, gave an insightful account of facing Laker in the nets. 'He had that wonderful gift of the ball that leaves the right-hand batsman. And he had flight. But he was a fairly lazy chap, really. You couldn't see him rolling up his sleeves and digging a hole in the ground. He'd get somebody else to do it and light up a cigarette.'

Laker's diffidence could be frustrating for his team–mates, and earned him a reputation for being wobbly under fire. Bizarrely, he missed more Tests than he played during the prime years of his career. Yet he was the quintessential English finger–spinner, landing the ball on a sixpence and spinning it like a sniper's bullet. Ted Dexter, who fielded at short-leg to Laker in his final series, was amazed to hear his off-breaks whirring through the air. 'When you saw him bowl,' Dexter wrote, 'you wondered why any off-spinner would contemplate bowling in a different fashion. He made it all look so simple.'

Laker set two records in 1956 that will probably stand for all time. He piled up 46 wickets in all, four more than anyone else has ever managed in an Ashes series. But his most astonishing feat was to take 19

Jim Laker in his *annus mirabilis* of 1956. If you include tour games, he dismissed 63 Australians at ten runs apiece. 'He was a fairly lazy chap, really,' said an England tour manager

'Well bowled, you bastard, now give me the bloody ball!'

Tony Lock tries to add to his single wicket as Jim Laker takes 19 at the other end

of them in one game at Old Trafford. This remains the most freakish individual performance in the history of the sport. The next best total by any bowler, Test or first-class, is 17. In statistical terms, Laker's match is out there in the furthest reaches of the cricketing galaxy, only a couple of light-years behind Bradman's batting average.

Some of Laker's victims at Old Trafford wanted their wickets to be credited to Bert Flack, the Lancashire groundsman. The surface was certainly treacherous. After rain, it turned as sticky as a 22-yard Mars Bar left in someone's pocket. But when the sun came out, the mud dried up and took on a powdery texture. One classic photograph shows the groundstaff sweeping the pitch and throwing up the kind of dust-storm more often seen in the American Midwest.

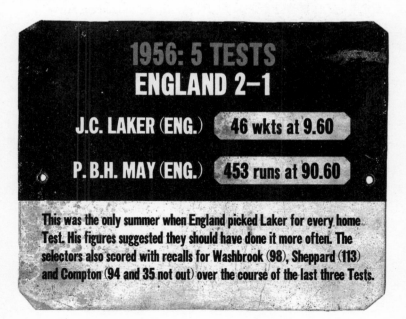

1956: 5 TESTS
ENGLAND 2–1

J.C. LAKER (ENG.)   46 wkts at 9.60

P. B.H. MAY (ENG.)   453 runs at 90.60

This was the only summer when England picked Laker for every home Test. His figures suggested they should have done it more often. The selectors also scored with recalls for Washbrook (98), Sheppard (113) and Compton (94 and 35 not out) over the course of the last three Tests.

'Let's have it straight,' wrote Bill O'Reilly after the match. 'This pitch is an absolute disgrace. What lies in store for Test cricket if the groundsmen are allowed to play the fool like this again?'

The appropriately named Flack was glad of diversions from the outside world. 'Thank God Nasser has taken over the Suez Canal,' he said. 'Otherwise, I'd be plastered over every front page like Marilyn Monroe.'

As Australia's No. 1 spinner and captain, Ian Johnson was damned twice over. Chosen ahead of Miller, he had been the safe appointment, but not the popular one. And now, according to support seamer Pat Crawford, 'Johnson couldn't get anything out of the players. Whereas the guys would have busted a gut for Keith. Mainly because they knew that, if he put his mind to it, he could do their job as well as they could.'

'No bugger got all 10 when I was bowling at the other end.'

Former England great Sydney Barnes on 'Laker's match'

Johnson lost many things on that 1956 tour, but not his sense of humour. When he lost that fatal toss at Old Trafford, he looked up to the pavilion and saw England's No. 3, the Reverend David Sheppard, still wearing his clerical robes. 'It isn't fair,' he remarked drily. 'Look who you've got on your side.'

BENAUD'S BENT-ARM ARMY

In Ashes cricket, one bad turn invariably leads to another. When England arrived in Australia for the 1958–59 tour, they were alarmed to find not one, not two, but four chuckers lined up against them. Like Old Testament blasphemers, Peter May's tourists were not so much bowled out as stoned to death.

The chucking crisis had been at least a decade in the making. Since the Second World War, the authorities had treated bent elbows rather as the Victorians did table-legs: they covered them up, and then they looked away. The result was that every team had a crop of suspect actions. May's England had Peter Loader, who was generally acknowledged to throw his bouncer and slower ball. And then there was Tony Lock, still firing in his yorkers with a suspicious snap.

But if England were infringing the letter of the law, Australia were ripping up the rulebook and stamping on the pieces. Nobody set the chuckometer spinning like their fast left-armer Ian Meckiff. In his account of the tour, May described seeing Meckiff for the first time as the players prepared for the Victoria state match. 'One of them . . . was throwing the ball at a batsman. This seemed an odd way for a bowler to limber up. A few minutes later he was out in the middle bowling to Peter Richardson with exactly the same action. I was fascinated.'

As a baseball pitcher, Meckiff would have walked many more batters than he struck out. 'One of the characteristics of the thrower is his wildness,' May wrote. 'But in this lies some of his effectiveness . . . There is no rhythm about the action, the line and pace are unpredictable – just a sudden jerk and the ball arrives.'

Meckiff – aka the sudden jerk – sent a murmur around the Brisbane crowd when he delivered his first ball of the series. Jim Laker was sitting next to a particularly irate spectator, the ousted Ray Lindwall, who described himself bitterly as 'the last of the straight-arm bowlers'. As Laker put it: 'One moment Meckiff would be a foot or two outside the leg stump, the next moment just as far away on the other side. "And this," thought poor old Lindwall, "is the man who is replacing me." I could see his point.'

When Meckiff took five wickets in the first Test, and nine in the second, Laker was quick to blame 'some sorry batting and dreadful strokes'. But this verdict took no account of a thrower's unpredictability. Classic strokeplayers like May and Colin Cowdrey based their whole game on a special talent for reading the pace and trajectory of the ball as it left the hand. A slight kink in the elbow was like a missing square in a crossword grid: it made the clues far harder to crack.

'Strike one, Strike two.'
Lindsay Hassett offers a baseball-style running commentary as he faces up to Tony Lock

In the first Test, Meckiff had occasional support from Jimmy Burke, an opening batsman and part-time spinner who cheerfully admitted to throwing his off-breaks. Burke's action was memorably likened by the cricket writer Ian Peebles to 'an officious policeman applying his truncheon to a particularly short offender's head'. And when the teams moved on to Sydney, Australia called a third dwarf-beater into their party. Keith Slater, who could turn his elbow to either pace or spin, had castled May in a warm-up match with a ball that Tom Graveney rated as faster than Lindwall at his best.

The most intimidating member of Australia's fearsome foursome only came in for the final two matches. Gordon Rorke was 6ft 5in tall and 15 stone, a handsome blond giant who answered to the nickname 'Lothar'. His action was not perhaps as bad as some of the others, but he made up for that by exploiting

'[like] an officious policeman applying his truncheon to a particularly short offender's head.'

Ian Peebles on the suspect action of off-spinner Jimmy Burke

the no-ball rule – which then required only the back foot to stay behind the line – and letting the ball go from closer to 18 yards than 22. The phenomenon of 'dragging' had long been a fast bowler's perk, but Rorke's extra height made him the ultimate drag-artist.

'I cannot believe that I would have taken readily to a helmet if helmets had then been in vogue,' wrote May. 'But if I had worn one ever, it would have been to Rorke. I knew that if he pitched it on the right spot, he would, as it were, hit double top and there would not be much I could do about it.'

The Adelaide Test was the battle of Rorke's lift. With a stock ball that arrived at chest height, he was horribly difficult to score off. Even Laker was prepared to admit that this fellow was a handful: 'The usual thing was to get five balls of an over so wide that you couldn't reach them with two bats tied together and then the fastest yorker you ever saw, right in the blockhole.'

On his next visit to Lord's, Cowdrey was accosted by a whiskery MCC colonel who insisted that the way to play Rorke was to get forward. 'We would have charged him like the Light Brigade!' he blustered. Cowdrey's response was a classic. 'I would have done, sir,' he replied, 'but I was afraid that he'd step on my toes.'

AND THEN THERE WERE NONE

May's team were not just thrown out by the bent-arm brigade, they were thrown into confusion. Some players wanted to make a formal protest; others took the view that if you were going to get beaten, you might as well go down with dignity. It was hardly as if England could claim a spotless record of sportsmanship.

Trevor Bailey, characteristically, was less concerned about rights and wrongs than wins and losses. He was the first to bring up the subject at a team meeting, arguing that: 'If nothing is done, [Meckiff] will win at least one Test match for Australia . . . If we are going to complain, we must do it before he becomes lethal.'

Bailey turned out to be spot-on, and both May and his manager Freddie Brown must have guessed it. Yet they decided to wave the issue through to the keeper. The decisive factor was May's lingering guilt about the previous series. 'We would have been accused of squealing,' he wrote. 'I knew what the Australians of 1956 thought about the pitches at Headingley and Old Trafford. They were understandably indignant . . . but they did not complain.'

The only time the Englishmen abandoned their philosophical air was at the final dinner of the tour. As they left, they told Bradman – still the most influential man in Australian cricket –

> 'Two laigs, please.'
> 'Blue-blooded ones, of course.'
> Ted Dexter takes guard on debut at Sydney, 1958–59; Australian wicketkeeper Wally Grout sledges him for his posh accent

that they would be submitting a very severe report to Lord's.

When it came to delivering threats, May was not exactly Marlon Brando. The sharpest thing about him was his side parting. But Bradman was an establishment man, especially since his knighthood, and he had no wish to fall out with MCC on account of a few lousy chuckers. Slowly and surely, he drew his plans against them.

From that point on, the offenders had all the life-expectancy of bit-part players in an episode of *Midsomer Murders*. The two off-spinners, Burke and Slater, never played another Test after the

Captains Benaud and May at the end of the 1958–59 series, won 4–0 by Australia, with several arms departing from the straight and narrow. Where was Darrell Hair when England needed him?

> **'In the cold light of everything, when it is looked at realistically, I must now concede that I was a chucker.'**
>
> **Ian Meckiff looks back**

winter of 1958–59 (victims, presumably, of the candlestick and the lead piping). Rorke's career ended when he contracted hepatitis in India a year later.

Bradman added another mark to Meckiff's card with a speech at Lord's in July 1960. 'If the doubtful bowling controversy goes unchecked, it could lead to an upheaval on the 1961 Australian tour of England,' he declared. 'What a tragedy it would be if our tour was threatened. It could lead to the greatest controversy in cricket history.' In just 18 months, Bradman had turned a full 180 degrees: from chief apologist to chief inquisitor. Even at 52, he was still pretty quick on his feet.

1958–59: 5 TESTS
AUSTRALIA 4–0

R. BENAUD (AUS.)   31 wkts at 18.83

A.K. DAVIDSON (AUS.)   24 wkts at 19.00 & 180 runs at 36.00

England reckoned they had been cheated out of the Ashes. It was true that the four chuckers – Meckiff, Rorke, Slater and Burke – took 29 wickets between them. On the other hand, Benaud and Davidson claimed a total of 55 without the slightest hint of a bent elbow.

In the end, Meckiff did not even make the squad. The reasoning was partly based on form, and partly on events at Lord's the previous summer, when a South African fast bowler was no-balled so often that he resorted to underarm. The only people more disappointed than Meckiff were Britain's sportswriters, who had been sharpening their pitchforks for a lynching.

Meckiff was picked for just one more Test match, and even that had the whiff of a stitch-up. At a cocktail reception before his final appearance, against South Africa in December 1963, the three selectors all looked twitchy and refused to talk to each other. Next morning, Meckiff was no-balled four times in his only over by umpire Colin Egar, who just happened to have travelled from Adelaide to Brisbane in the company of Bradman.

Conspiracy or coincidence? No one really knows, though the journalist Dick Whitington was convinced that Richie Benaud, the Australian captain, was in on the plot. According to Whitington, Benaud was well aware 'that Meckiff's inclusion on the 1964 tour of England would hardly assist Australia's chances of retaining the Ashes'.

Meckiff had one small consolation: a fat cheque from a newspaper in exchange for his life story. He produced some colourful copy, claiming that the no-ball call had hit him 'like a dagger in the back'. But his parting shot was brave and honest, if a couple of years overdue: 'In the cold light of everything, when it is looked at realistically, I must now concede that I was a chucker.'

TOTAL
TEAM SPIRIT

The 1958–59 Ashes came as quite a shock for May and his darling buds. Up until that point, England's debonair captain had gone three years unbeaten. Yet even after losing the series 4–0, May still rated the tour as a personal success. 'At the end of it,' he wrote, 'England and Australia were still speaking.'

May saw the whole series as a sporting morality play. He believed that England's cheek-turning self-sacrifice had saved the game from a second Bodyline crisis. But the captain's stoicism had its downsides. For one thing, England had just waved farewell to their precious urnful of dust for the whole of the 1960s. And for another, May's triumphant rival was about to overtake him in the Golden Boy stakes.

Cricket fans now know Richie Benaud as the Yoda of televised sport – a wizened, Confucian figure whose sparse commentary lets the images speak for themselves. But in his younger days Benaud was an exuberant, free-spirited performer. He wore his shirt unbuttoned halfway to the waist, leapt like a dolphin in the gully, and encouraged his players to perform handstands (or at least high-fives) whenever a wicket fell. This was more than male bonding, Benaud claimed – it was 'total team spirit'.

Jim Laker was just one of many senior pros who reacted sniffily to

> **'Don't bother shutting it, son, you won't be out there long enough.'**
>
> Fred Trueman as a new Australian batsman closes the gate on his way out of the pavilion at Lord's, early 1960s

Ring of fire: Alan Davidson bowls through the pain barrier at Lord's after smothering his stiff back in liniment. As he put it: 'When I started sweating, it started to slip down and burn the orifice'

such vulgar antics. He grumbled that: 'Almost in the manner of the professional soccer player, [Benaud] would rush around, all but embracing those concerned. I'm all for enthusiasm in its proper place, but I felt this behaviour did little for the dignity of cricket.' But then, Laker's reaction was typical of a man who defined celebration as a hitch of the trousers and a handshake. As Alan Ross wrote in *The Times*, 'Even when bowling out 19 Australians in a Test match . . . his demeanour implied that the whole thing was a fearful chore.'

The 1961 Ashes were another success story for Benaud, the skipper who skipped for delight. His right-hand man was the left-arm seamer Alan Davidson, a fine bowler whose only foible was his rampant hypochondria. Benaud became expert at wringing one extra over out of him, often going so far as to help him out of his sweater if he baulked.

Davidson outdid himself during the Lord's Test (which became known as 'The Battle of the Ridge' after surveyors discovered a raised area at one end of the pitch). He had come into the match with a stiff back, which he smothered in Capsulin, an industrial-strength version of Deep Heat. As the chemicals got to work, his stride lengthened, and the ball started lifting nastily off the ridge.

'It was stuff they used to warm up an area of the body,' Davidson recalled, 'and, well, it really worked. When I started sweating, it started to slip down and burn the orifice. People said:

Sting in the tail: Benaud bowls May round his legs to clinch the 1961 Old Trafford Test and the Ashes. Benaud's old mate Davidson joked that his OBE stood for 'Other Bastards' Efforts'

"Christ, you got stuck into them." And I told them: "Well, if you'd had your backside on fire, you'd've done the same.'"

If that was an odd way to win a Test, the same could be said of Old Trafford, where Benaud despatched May and Dexter with the unheard-of tactic of bowling leg-spin from around the wicket. As the Derbyshire fast bowler Harold Rhodes once remarked to him: 'If you put your head in a bucket of slops, Benordy, you'd come up with a mouthful of diamonds.'

WHEN TED MET FRED

'Sexual intercourse began in 1963,' according to Philip Larkin's poem 'Annus Mirabilis', 'Between the end of the Chatterley ban and the Beatles' first LP.' The sense of liberation extended far beyond Carnaby Street. Within cricket's cloistered world, the abolition of the old gentlemen/players distinction – accomplished during that same heady spring of 1963 – must have resonated like the fall of the Berlin Wall. No more 'shamateurs', no more professionals' dressing-rooms, no more Titmus, F.J.

But while the trappings may have changed, the old social divides persisted: middle-class, privately educated batsmen; working-class, predominantly northern, bowlers. In the mid-1960s, these worlds collided in the shape of Ted Dexter, England's aristocratic captain, and the darkly mutinous Fred Trueman. Lord Ted and Fiery Fred – as they were known to the tabloids – were the two best cricketers in the world at the time. They were also a pair of charismatic, overbearing men, who would have dominated the 1962–63 Ashes if they hadn't spent the tour bickering like fishwives.

> **'Kid yourself it's a Sunday, Rev., and put your hands together.'**
> Fred Trueman to a butter-fingered David Sheppard

England took a 1–0 lead, thanks to Trueman's eight wickets at Melbourne. After that they picked the wrong teams and the wrong fights, allowing Australia to escape with a drawn series. As Trueman himself put it: 'A lot of tactical mistakes were made – vital ones – and

Dexter drives, 1964. According to *Wisden*, 'a thrill went round the ground when he strode majestically to the wicket and bowlers feared the punishment they were about to receive'

I reckon that Ted Dexter must take the blame . . . He had more theory than Darwin, but little practical experience to back it up.'

Trueman produced two famous sledges on that tour – both directed at members of his own team. When the Reverend David Sheppard put down a series of chances at slip, Trueman burst out: 'Kid yourself it's a Sunday, Rev., and put your hands together.' Later on, Colin Cowdrey made the same mistake, and compounded the error by letting the ball fly straight through him for four. Cowdrey raised his hand and said: 'Sorry, Fred, I should have crossed my legs.' To which Trueman replied 'No, but your mother should have.'

If an Australian had delivered a crack like that, it would have brought the house down. Among Dexter's class–conscious tourists,

The Rev. David Sheppard was a cultured strokeplayer who went on to become Bishop of Liverpool. His nickname in Conservative political circles was 'The Turbulent Priest'

the joke carried a dangerous whiff of rebellion. Trueman wrote that it 'helped as much as anything to £50 being subtracted from my good conduct bonus'.

Dexter and Trueman found themselves at loggerheads again during the Headingley Test of 1964. As England pressed for a first-innings lead, Trueman insisted that he could bounce the tailenders out. Dexter was equally adamant that he should aim at the stumps. The upshot was that Peter Burge stormed to a match-winning 160, hooking boundary after boundary through a vacant square-leg.

This was the opposite of team-work. 'I blame Ted Dexter,

the skipper, for what happened,' wrote Trueman, with his usual sense of personal responsibility. Perhaps Dexter should have accepted this as an argument he was never going to win, and set the leg-side trap accordingly. But Trueman was equally guilty of overestimating his own potency. He was 33 now, but too self-satisfied to realise that his pace was beginning to wane. Ten years later, that same dogmatic streak would characterise his radio career on *Test Match Special*, where his catchphrase became: 'I joost don't know what's going off out there.'

1962–63: 5 TESTS
DRAWN 1–1

A.K. DAVIDSON (AUS.) — 24 wkts at 20.00 & 158 runs at 22.57

K.F. BARRINGTON (ENG.) — 582 runs at 72.75

Trueman's outswing powered England into the lead at Melbourne. He insisted that they would have won the next game as well if only Dexter had accepted the need for two spinners. Instead, Fred Titmus took seven wickets from one end while the seamers toiled fruitlessly from the other, and Australia drew level.

THE DREARIEST DECADE

If Ted Dexter had played today, he would have been a colossal star, on a par with the Bothams and Flintoffs. He was one of the great British all-rounders – a man who played golf off scratch, stood for Parliament, and once flew himself around the world. So far, so *Boy's Own*. But when Dexter was appointed England captain, the job seemed to transform him from Biggles into Dan Daren't. His leadership was duller than the dourest professional's. Over three years in the job, he drew more often than Jesse James.

Dexter was not alone. A niggardly spirit seemed to infect the whole decade; in Ashes cricket, the 1960s were anything but swinging. The disease really took hold during the final Test of 1962–63, when even that natural adventurer Richie Benaud put his own unbeaten record ahead of the spectators. After Australia refused to chase 241 at just over three runs per over, Keith Miller lambasted 'The Battle of the Spineless Skippers'.

Australia's next two Ashes captains were worse, much worse. Bob Simpson and Bill Lawry were both opening batsmen, and brought that same over-my-dead-body spirit to the top job. Indeed, Lawry was so tenacious that he sometimes seemed to be gripped by rigor mortis; the English reporter Ian Wooldridge described him as 'a corpse with pads on'.

Simpson's definitive innings came at Old Trafford in 1964, the Test after the Dexter–Trueman bust-up at Headingley. He

Colin Cowdrey catches Neil Hawke to make Fred Trueman the first bowler to 300 Test wickets. Asked if he thought his record would be beaten, Trueman replied: 'I don't know, but whoever does it will be bloody tired'

1964: 5 TESTS
AUSTRALIA 1–0

G.D. McKENZIE (AUS.) — 29 wkts at 22.55

R.B. SIMPSON (AUS.) — 458 runs at 76.33

Peter Burge hooked and pulled his way to 160 brilliant runs at Headingley. With the help of a wagging tail, he lifted Australia from 178 for seven to a match-winning 389. At The Oval, Neil Hawke became Trueman's 300th Test victim.

'A corpse with pads on.'

Ian Wooldridge on the gritty Australian captain Bill Lawry

won the toss and set himself to bat England out of the match. By the end of the second day, he had made an unbeaten 265 off almost as many overs. It was mind-numbing stuff – reminiscent, as one writer observed, of that other great Simpson who discovered chloroform.

Dexter blamed the concept of the Ashes for encouraging a safety-first approach. 'If they were abolished and each man paid £1,000 for winning, there would have been a result,' he claimed, after that infamous Sydney Test of 1962–63. Dexter was right that Australia made urn-retention their priority throughout the 1960s. But England were in no position to talk. They had their own

No Ashes yet for England – but piles of sawdust and a series squared. 'Deadly' Derek Underwood traps Inverarity lbw at a soggy Oval, August 1968. The England players clustered round the bat are Graveney, Edrich, Dexter, Cowdrey, Knott, Snow, Brown, Milburn and D'Oliveira

1965–66: 5 TESTS
DRAWN 1–1

R.M. COWPER (AUS.)   493 runs at 82.16

W.M. LAWRY (AUS.)   592 runs at 84.57

M.J.K. Smith's tourists emulated Dexter's, four years previously, by taking the lead and then letting it slip. This series was all about batsmen named Bob. Bob Barber's 185 set up England's win, Bob Simpson's 225 helped Australia equalise, and Bob Cowper's 307 made the Ashes safe at Melbourne.

drag-anchors in Geoff Boycott and Ken Barrington, both of whom suffered the indignity of being dropped for slow scoring. Boycott, the arch-blocker, was all tortoise and not much hair.

At least England ended the 1960s in style. The final Test of 1968, played at The Oval, produced more entertainment in one crazy hour than the rest of the series put together. The drama began when Australia were 86 for five at lunch on the final day, facing near-certain defeat. Then a massive thunderstorm swept across the ground, flooding the outfield so thoroughly that the players started packing their bags. Half-an-hour later, the sun came out and the mopping-up operation began. But this was no modern scene of hover covers and mechanised water-hogs. As the groundsmen went to work with their sponges, hundreds of fans rolled up their sleeves and trouser legs and got busy with towels and blankets.

Under current ground regulations, the intruders would all have been

> **'What's wrong with you, Lawry? Have you taken the pill?'**
>
> A barracker reacts to slow scoring, Sydney, 1965–66

ejected. In those more innocent times, they were rewarded with a 75-minute cliff-hanger. Derek Underwood was a past master at exploiting a damp pitch, and he swept through the tail, finally removing stubborn opener John Inverarity with just five minutes left on the clock. The flotilla of handkerchiefs had carried England to a famous victory.

If Underwood won the Test, Basil D'Oliveira's 158 changed the world. D'Oliveira's innings won him a place on the following winter's tour to South Africa – the same country he had escaped a decade earlier. And when the leaders of the apartheid regime questioned his right, as a Cape Coloured émigré, to play against their monochrome champions, the concept of a sporting boycott was born.

> ## 'I have on occasions taken a quite reasonable dislike to the Australians.'
> Ted Dexter looks back in anger, 1972

DEFENDER OF THE REALM

There must have been a few readers suppressing a giggle when a daily newspaper trailed its new coaching series in 1985: 'Brighter Cricket With Geoff Boycott'. Those giggles turned to guffaws when the opening chapter was published: 'No. 1: The Backward Defensive Stroke'.

Boycott's batting has attracted many adjectives, but 'bright' was rarely one of them. Indeed England dropped him in 1967 after he scored 246 in almost 10 hours against India at Headingley, in defiance of MCC's desire for bells and whistles. As Boycott wrote of the 'brighter cricket' slogan, 'it sounds fine and nobody challenges it as a philosophy until the "brighter" team collapses in a strangled heap'.

The selectors' argument was that Boycott's first loyalty was to himself, not to the team. Whether true or not, this vastly underestimated his value. Only 20 of his 108 Tests ended in defeat for England, mostly when he failed. When the team stopped in Ceylon (now Sri Lanka) on their way to Australia in 1965–66, they were asked to state the purpose of their visit. Fourteen of them put 'To play cricket,' Bob Barber wrote 'Holiday,' and Boycott just put 'Business'.

Barber and Boycott made a contrasting opening pair. Barber was a free-spirited Cambridge graduate, backed by family money, who would

> **'The only fellow I've met who fell in love with himself at a young age and has remained faithful ever since.'**
>
> Dennis Lillee on Boycott

'You have done for Australian cricket what the Boston Strangler did for door-to-door salesmen.'

Telegram sent to Geoff Boycott after a
very slow 50 at Perth, 1978–79

throw his wicket away if he felt like a bit of sunbathing. He hit the first ball he faced on that 1965–66 tour back over Garth McKenzie's head for four. Yet Barber, surprisingly, became a great friend and ally of Boycott's. 'There was this idea that Geoff, because he was determined to get on, was selfish,' he said. 'Well, I can tell you, there was an awful lot of selfishness around then.'

Barber even forgave Boycott for running him out, another common gripe within the dressing-room. While Denis Compton was the original kamikaze runner – a man whose calls 'should be treated as no more than a basis for negotiations', according to Trevor Bailey – Boycott wasn't far behind. To paraphrase the ancient joke about women drivers, he didn't have many accidents but he saw plenty.

The most famous instance came at Trent Bridge in 1977. Boycott had just returned to the England side after a three-year sulk, caused by the selectors' preference for Mike Denness as captain. Stuck on 13 after a long crease-occupation, he pushed the ball back to Jeff Thomson and called for a crazy single. Not only was his partner run out by yards, but that partner was Derek Randall, darling of the Nottingham crowd.

Boycott stood at the far end with one hand over his face and his bat abandoned on the ground. 'I have never felt so wretched on a cricket field,' he wrote. But he rallied to score 107 – 'my hardest innings, physically, mentally and emotionally' – then added an unbeaten 80 in the second innings to seal England's victory. In the next match at Headingley, he was at it again, only this time the crowd was all on his side as he brought up his 100th first-class hundred. As the *Wisden* editor Matthew Engel wrote: 'We sometimes argue about the cricketer we

Boycott runs out the local hero, 1977. The _Guardian_ quipped: '[Myra] Hindley . . . only participated in some of the grisliest murders of the 20th century, whereas Geoffrey ran out Derek Randall at Trent Bridge'

would choose to bat for our life. (Consensus answer: Bradman for your life, Boycott for his own.)'

The best Boycott story of all is probably apocryphal, but worth retelling nonetheless. It dates from Australia in 1970–71, when England were often confounded by Johnny Gleeson, a spinner who emulated Jack Iverson's grip and mysterious delivery style.

According to the tale, Boycott was batting with Basil D'Oliveira, who mentioned between overs that he had finally found a way of differentiating Gleeson's leg-break from his off-break. Boycott just grunted and replied: 'Oh, aye, I worked that out a fortnight ago.' Then he pointed to the England dressing-room and said: 'But don't tell those buggers up there.'

REIGN OF FIRE

1970-1987

STREET FIGHTING MEN

The phenomenon of sledging was almost universal in top-level cricket. Don Bradman once said that the only Tests he had known 'without verbal aggression' were during the 1932–33 Ashes, when the savagery of Bodyline struck both teams dumb. But as the 20th century drew on, strong language and backchat grew more prevalent in all walks of life. Soon the players needed a term to describe what they said to each other in the heat of battle (and then tried to forget about in the snug of the bar).

> **'So how's your wife and my kids?'**
> **'The wife's fine – the kids are retarded.'**
> Rod Marsh and Ian Botham – sledge and counter-sledge, late 1970s

Oddly, the phrase was coined not on the field, but at a barbecue after a Sheffield Shield game in Adelaide in the early 1970s. When New South Wales fast bowler Grahame Corling made a coarse remark to John Benaud, embarrassing his team-mate's female companion, Benaud replied that Corling was about as 'subtle as a sledgehammer'. The verb 'to sledge' soon caught on. And once Ian Chappell had taken over the Australian captaincy, in February 1971, there were plenty of opportunities to use it.

Chappell's appointment for the final match of the 1970–71 series gave cricket a sharp new edge. Throughout the 1960s, Ashes Tests had resembled chess matches in which both captains made probing early moves, then sat back and settled for a draw. Under

Ian Chappell: his grandfather, Vic Richardson, was the only
senior member of Australia's 1932–33 team who wanted to copy
Jardine's Bodyline tactics. 'Forty years later . . . I chose, like
my granddad would have done, to stick it up them'

Chappell, they became red-blooded fistfights, littered with more
bouncers than an Oscars after-party.

The Chappell regime was built on fast bowling, fierce verbals
and freakish facial hair. After one finger-pointing bust-up in
Christchurch, New Zealand's press dubbed his team 'The Ugly
Australians'. Yet Chappell was more Dr Jekyll than Mr Hyde (unless
he saw the batsman trying to influence the umpire, which produced
a sudden transformation). He preferred to stand with arms folded
at first slip, leaving Dennis Lillee, the Zapata-moustached enforcer,
to do his dirty work for him.

The cerebral England captain Mike Brearley once said: 'Playing
against a team with Ian Chappell as captain turns a cricket match
into gang warfare.' These Australians intimidated opponents both
with the way they looked – Lillee and his sidekick Rod Marsh
could have passed for Hell's Angels – and with the things they said.
As Lillee admitted: 'I'm just so pent up against the batsman that

'Boycott?' 'Bounce the c∗∗∗.' 'Edrich?' 'Bounce the c∗∗∗.' 'Willis?' 'Slog the c∗∗∗.' 'Underwood?' 'Bloody tight. Hard to get away. Slog the c∗∗∗.'

Ian Chappell addresses an Australian team meeting, 1970s

I let him have a bit of my tongue as he goes.' Marsh was equally garrulous, and funny with it. On one occasion in the late 1970s, he greeted Ian Botham with the words: 'So how's your wife and my kids?' Botham's reply: 'The wife's fine – the kids are retarded.'

Chappell's pre-Test meetings were nothing if not direct. The leg-spinner Kerry O'Keeffe recalled that: 'Ian would go through the other team by name. "Boycott?" "Bounce the c∗∗∗." "Edrich?" "Bounce the c∗∗∗." "Willis?" "Slog the c∗∗∗." "Underwood?" "Bloody tight. Hard to get away. Slog the c∗∗∗."'

These were cricketers who smashed sixes, wore jeans and staged drinking contests on intercontinental flights. No wonder the fans loved them. Chappell's first Ashes tour as captain, in 1972, broke all records for box-office income. For Chappell himself, the highlight of that trip was a boozy stay at London's Waldorf Hotel, where the team mixed with rock stars and actors. One regular visitor to the hotel bar was Mick Jagger. If Chappell could have been the model for the Rolling Stones' 'Street Fighting Man', then Lillee clearly had 'Sympathy For The Devil'.

EVERY QUICK FOR HIMSELF

Aggression in the early 1970s was not a one-way street. At Sydney in 1970–71, the English fast bowler John Snow caused a sensation. In the space of 15 minutes, he felled a tailender, started a riot, and prompted the first walk-off in Test history. Considering that England regained the Ashes three days later, Snow had a pretty exceptional week.

Snow's autobiography bore the apposite title *Cricket Rebel*. The son of a clergyman, he was an enigmatic, wild-haired figure who would have looked more at home fronting Pink Floyd than the England attack. Off the field, he wrote poetry and had a reputation for surliness. On it, he was the original nasty fastie. When Geoff Boycott had the temerity to goad him in a county match in 1969, Snow went round the wicket and broke Boycott's hand with what wicketkeeper Jim Parks called: 'The best bouncer I have ever seen in my life.'

Snow aimed his short ball at the batsman's front armpit rather than their head. This was a canny tactic, because whenever the umpires warned him for intimidation, he would reply indignantly that he hadn't been bowling bouncers. After one such debate during the second Test, umpire Lou Rowan snapped: 'Somebody's bowling them from this end and it's not me.'

If Snow's tactics were unflinching, one could rarely say the same about his victims. In that fourth Test at Sydney, he gleaned a match-winning seven for 40 – effectively eight, as Australian fast man Garth McKenzie had to retire hurt with blood streaming from his mouth. Then, when he bowled at Terry Jenner in the final Test,

'I'm not afraid of leaving a trail of fractures among the opposition – a finger, a thumb, a whole right hand and one foot on the latest count. After all, that's what I'm there for.'

England fast bowler John Snow, 1971

came the ball that raised hell. This was one of those tipping-points in cricket history. While the fast bowlers' union had never been totally reliable, tailenders had at least made some sort of effort to look after each other. Now the credo had switched to 'Every man for himself, and the devil take the slowest.'

This new generation of pacemen did not bother to disguise their intentions. After taking 31 wickets on the 1970–71 tour, Snow wrote: 'I'm not afraid of leaving a trail of fractures among the opposition – a finger, a thumb, a whole right hand and one foot on the latest count. After all, that's what I'm there for. Not to inflict deliberate injury, of course, but to rough up a batsman, make them apprehensive and destroy their confidence. I never let them forget the game is played with a very hard ball.'

Lillee clearly learned a great deal from Snow in that series. When he delivered his own mission statement, on the eve of the 1974–75 Ashes, it sounded uncannily similar. 'I try to hit a batsman in the rib cage when I bowl a purposeful bouncer,' Lillee wrote, 'and I want it to hurt so much that the batsman doesn't want to face me any more . . . not many batsmen recover from a really good bouncer.' The warcry had been sounded.

BOTTLES AND BEERCANS

The clouds that unleashed the Snow storm had been building all series, as he traded short balls with his opposite number, Alan 'Froggy' Thomson. After ducking one Thomson bouncer, Snow went up to him at a cocktail reception in Adelaide, ran a finger along his hair, and asked him where he wanted it parted.

But poor Jenner could hardly fight Snow with fire; he was a humble leg-spinner (and, later, the coach who turned Shane Warne into a global superstar). Going in No. 9, Jenner found Snow's first three balls all lifting awkwardly towards his ribs. He squeezed the first away for a single, wriggled out of the path of the second, and tried to duck under the third. That was a mistake: the ball struck him such a heavy blow on the scalp that it rebounded towards cover.

The umpire, Lou Rowan, made no comment as the players rushed round, helped the bloodied Jenner to his feet and escorted him off the field. Then, as Snow prepared to bowl again, he called: 'Just a minute, John. I am not impressed by your performance and I am giving you a first warning.'

Snow whirled around and retorted: 'That's the first bouncer I've bowled this over – your blokes have been bowling seven.' Ray Illingworth joined him, and while the pair of them stood rowing with Rowan, a dozen beercans flew over the fence and landed around the fine-leg boundary. Eventually, Snow finished the over, snatched his hat and stalked down to his fielding position adjacent to Sydney's infamous Hill. As he moved close to the fence, making provocative 'Come on, then' gestures to the hecklers, a middle-aged

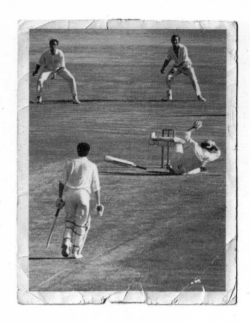

Head case: Terry Jenner is felled by a bouncer from England's John Snow, Sydney, 1971. Like Bert Oldfield's cracked skull some forty years earlier (see page 110), the blow nearly provoked a riot

drunk leant over the pickets and grabbed him by the shirt. 'What the hell do you think you're doing?' yelled Snow, pushing his assailant back. But there was no answer. As Snow said later: 'He couldn't speak – he was stoned.'

A second volley of bottles and beercans now burst from the crowd. Ray Illingworth, the England captain, ran over to draw Snow away and signalled to his team that they were leaving the field. It was a scene of total confusion. 'What do we do now?' Lillee asked Chappell. 'We stay here until we are told to do something different,' his captain replied. Up in the commentary box, Bill Lawry turned to Richie Benaud in triumph over a wager, crowing 'Pay up, Benordy, they've forfeited.'

Rowan now entered the England dressing-room and said: 'What's going on, Mr Illingworth? Is your team coming back on the field or are you forfeiting the match?' With the Ashes on the line,

> **'I have seen people hit by bottles and it makes a bloody mess of them.'**
> **Ray Illingworth justifies his Sydney walk-off**

1970–71: 6 TESTS
ENGLAND 2–0

G. BOYCOTT (ENG.) | 657 runs at 93.86

J.A. SNOW (ENG.) | 31 wkts at 22.84

Snow's great series reinforced the theory that the best way of winning a series in Australia was to unearth a fearsome fast bowler. With Australia 1–0 down going into the final Test, Lawry was ruthlessly dumped as captain and replaced by Ian Chappell. But Australia lost that game too.

there was only one response. The outfield was cleared of some 40 beercans and a few stubby beer bottles, and the game went on.

England eventually regained the urn, but they had to finish the job without Snow. He had bowled just two overs when he misjudged a spiralling catch and spiked his hand on that same picket fence in front of the Hill. It was a busy week for the SCG's medics: just like Jenner, and the unfortunate sightscreen attendant who was concussed by a beercan, Snow had to be carted off to hospital.

When Snow finally came to write the story of a long and bolshie career, he saved his greatest scorn for Lou Rowan. 'I have never come across another umpire so stubborn, lacking in humour, unreasonable and utterly unable to distinguish between a delivery short of a length and a genuine bouncer which goes through head high.' Snow also noted that Rowan had failed to give England a single lbw decision in the whole series.

> **'I didn't know they stacked crap that high.'**
> The crowd barracks England's 6ft 5in fast bowler Bob Willis, 1970–71

THE SPORES OF WRATH

Sandwiched between the John Snow riot and the Jeff Thomson apocalypse, the 1972 Ashes are now best remembered for introducing a new word to cricket's lexicon: fusarium. This microscopic fungus was the bogeyman as Australia went down to a nine-wicket defeat at Headingley. The weekend before the game, freak thunderstorms had infected the ground with its invisible spores – or so the authorities claimed.

The Australians were not convinced. Ian Chappell pointed out that fusarium is supposed to thrive in temperatures above 75 degrees Fahrenheit, which would represent a positive heatwave in Leeds. His brother Greg wrote: 'It was uncanny that it only attacked a strip 22 yards by eight feet and the rest of the ground was perfectly healthy. Quite a coincidence, too, that England had selected two spinners for the match.' The day before the Test, the Australian opening batsman Keith Stackpole bounced a ball on the already crumbling pitch, and saw the rebound rise no more than toe-high. He compared it to the desert areas of Western Australia. Older observers were reminded of Jim Laker's 1956 sandbanks.

Australia won what should have been an important toss, but their off-spinner Ashley Mallett was no match for Derek Underwood at his deadliest. After the game, their manager Ray Steele told his players: 'We were dudded, we all know that, but we won't be whingeing about it to anyone, least of all the press. Anyone whines about the Headingley wicket and I'll come down on you like a ton of bricks.'

The classical action of the great Dennis Lillee. The comedian Eric Morecambe was more impressed by Lillee's moustache: 'The last time I saw anything like that on a top lip, the whole herd had to be destroyed'

Though Chappell went home without the Ashes, he knew he had the makings of a winning side. Most importantly, he had an irresistible spearhead. Dennis Lillee took 31 wickets in the series, a record for an Australian in England. With his Dick Dastardly antics and bounding run, Lillee was the most theatrical of cricketers. The only way he could psych himself up to top speed was to focus on how much he hated batsmen. 'I treat them like faceless, meaningless thieves,' he wrote.

The son of a truck driver from Perth, Lillee also revelled in his image as a backwoodsman. At a reception at Buckingham Palace, he distinguished himself by greeting the Queen with a hearty 'G'day'. When Chappell remarked to Ray Steele: 'You wouldn't believe what Dennis said when I introduced him to the Queen,' Steele replied: 'Yes I would. "G'day" – exactly the same as he said to the bloody Duke!'

'G'day, howya going?'

Lillee meets Queen Elizabeth II, 1972

While this remains the most famous example of *lèse-majesté* by an Australian cricketer, it is not the only one. After play at Lord's in 1968, Ashley Mallett remembers 'talking among a group of fellow players when I saw from a distance of about ten yards away a rather elegant-looking woman approaching. My short-sightedness had never really embarrassed me before, but I called out, "I say my dear, will you not join us here?"' The ensuing silence was even more awkward than Mallett's gangling approach to the bowling crease.

But the blue riband must go to another Western Australian fast bowler who was never afraid to call a spade a shovel. Standing in the line-up at Lord's in 1981, Rodney Hogg bowed respectfully as Her Majesty passed by. Then, as Kim Hughes proceeded with the introductions, Hogg leaned forward, followed her progress for a couple of seconds, and remarked – slightly too loudly – 'Nice legs for an old Sheila.'

1972: 5 TESTS
DRAWN 2–2

D.K. LILLEE (AUS.) | 31 wkts at 17.67

R.A.L. MASSIE (AUS.) | 23 wkts at 17.78

After Bob Massie had given Australia the lead at Lord's with his extraordinary 16 for 137 on Test debut, Derek Underwood retorted with 10 for 82 on Headingley's infamous 'Fusarium' pitch. Bizarrely, Massie would play only two more Tests after this series, and dropped out of his state team within 18 months.

THE KILLING FIELDS

Mention the 1974–75 Ashes series to some of England's survivors and, even now, a look of distant horror enters their eyes. It is like dealing with victims of shellshock. Were Dennis Lillee and Jeff Thomson the most fearsome fast-bowling outfit of them all? In Ashes history, the answer is undoubtedly 'Yes'. Perhaps the four-pronged West Indian pace attacks were more relentless. Certainly they bowled more bouncers per over. But no one has ever propelled a cricket ball faster than Thomson. He was a one-man sonic boom.

The irony of 1974–75 is that England were not expecting too much of a hurry-up from the Australian bowlers. Lillee was on his way back from spinal stress fractures, which had required him to spend six weeks of the 1973–74 season entombed in plaster from his buttocks to his neck. Thomson's single Test had produced figures of 19–1–110–0 against Pakistan – the result of playing with a broken toe.

England, now under Scottish-born captain Mike Denness, started the tour overflowing with confidence (some might say complacency). They were so cocky that they left the 33-year-old Snow at home – presumably because of his general contrariness – and still romped through their warm-ups, winning two and drawing the other two comfortably.

> **'Ashes to Ashes, dust to dust, if Lillee don't get you, Thommo must.'**
> Crowd chant during the 1974–75 Ashes series

The gruesome twosome: Australian cricket writer Gideon Haigh remarked: 'Lillee and Thomson remain a combination to conjure with, as sinister in England as Burke and Hare, or Bismarck and Tirpitz'

This time, though, it was England's turn to be 'dudded'. If Thomson bowled innocuously for Queensland, it was only because he was deliberately running at what he called 'half rat power'. The whole thing was a set-up. In the first Test at Brisbane, Denness's men ran into the biggest ambush since the Trojan War.

Less than an hour into England's first innings, Thomson scored his first casualty. His inswinging bouncer shattered the thumb – and the nerve – of Dennis Amiss, the Warwickshire opener who was then shaping to be the next great England batsman. 'Several times I walked to the middle beaten before I started,' Amiss would later confess. 'The bat

> **'It doesn't worry me in the least to see the batsman hurt, rolling around screaming and blood on the pitch.'**
> Jeff Thomson, 1974

in my hand seemed superfluous against these two . . . batting was a complete misery.'

Thomson never said a word on the field, unlike the reliably foul-mouthed Lillee. But he did enjoy posing as a cold-eyed killer, even if it was largely for the media's benefit. 'I enjoy hitting a batsman more than getting him out,' he told one interviewer in June 1974. 'It doesn't worry me in the least to see the batsman hurt, rolling around screaming and blood on the pitch.' He also claimed to have struck a grade opponent such a hideous blow in the eye that the poor man spent a week in intensive care.

While no batsman was quite so badly maimed in 1974–75, there was still a frequent shuttle service between Australia's cricket grounds and her hospitals. The Englishmen joked that the chair containing the next batsman was 'the condemned cell'. Most of them felt relieved if Thomson only broke their stumps, rather than their bones.

> **'The injury did confirm my earlier statement that I could play Thommo with my cock.'**
>
> **England's David Lloyd takes a fast one in the box**

If some were wondering whether Lillee was past his best, he soon blew that canard out of the water. John Edrich sustained three fractures off Lillee – one to his hand at Brisbane; two in his ribs at Sydney. One of the bravest men ever to pull on the three lions, Edrich was hospitalised first ball by a Lillee skidder. But he returned to make an unbeaten 33 in two-and-a-half hours, ignoring the pain in his side and moving rigidly into line.

The most sickening blow of all – though no bones were broken – was probably the one Thomson inflicted on David Lloyd's groin protector at Perth, smashing this manifestly inadequate piece of pink plastic into smithereens. Lloyd had to be carried off, and only managed to resume his innings the next day. Ever the wise guy, Lloyd joked afterwards: 'The injury did confirm my earlier statement that I could play Thommo with my cock.'

Years later, when Middlesex seamer Mike Selvey incapacitated Lloyd in similar fashion at Lord's, he popped into the dressing-room to commiserate. Lloyd just grinned and told him: 'After Thommo, you were a pleasure.'

THE ULTIMATE WANG-ER

Thomson was a natural, pure and simple. No coaching for him; no 3-D analysis or scientific fine-tuning. As he himself put it, 'I just shuffle up and go wang.' It just so happened that his 'wang' was a marvel of biomechanical efficiency.

As he moved into his javelin-style delivery stride, Thomson kicked his front toe up chin-high, and dragged his right hand around behind his body until his knuckles were virtually scraping the turf. Then came the crash of the left leg, like the uncoiling of a giant spring. For the batsman, the ball appeared horribly late – 1/20th of a second before release, according to one calculation. After another 1/3rd of a second, it was fizzing past his nose (if he was lucky).

England's young fast bowler Bob Willis was simultaneously mesmerised and terrified. This was all so different to his own wild-eyed, high-kneed approach, which was likened by one writer to 'a 1914 biplane tied up with elastic bands trying vainly to take off'.

> **'I couldn't wait to have a crack at 'em. I thought: "Stuff that stiff upper lip crap. Let's see how stiff it is when it's split."'**
> Australian fast bowler Jeff Thomson looks back, 1986

Willis admitted that he could not even see many of the balls sent down by 'the nuclear explosion that is Jeff Thomson', and wondered aloud why more people did not bowl in a similar way. But this comment underestimated Thomson's extraordinary physical gifts. He combined great strength and co-ordination with such flexibility that he could pull his ankles up behind his ears.

The unique
slinging action
of Australia's
Jeff Thomson.
'I don't try to
be Joe Blow,
the super-stud –
it just happens'

Even Thomson's own team-mates were shocked when he bowled his first over at Brisbane. Already standing some 35 yards from the bat, Marsh had to jump high to his right to reach one rocket that lifted off a length. 'Hell, that hurt,' he drawled. 'But I love it.'

It must have been some small relief to England that Lillee, the senior bowler, always got the advantage of the wind. Lillee was not as quick as he had been in 1972, by his own admission, but he was more accurate and still capable of the odd thunderbolt. There was one horrible moment at Sydney when tailender Geoff Arnold lost sight of a short ball that exploded off the pitch. Arnold stood stock-still, like a rabbit hypnotised by a swaying cobra, as the ball brushed his face, climbed over the leaping Marsh and smashed into the sightscreen on the first bounce.

'Good Lord, he's knocked old George off his horse now.'
England's Geoff Arnold as Thommo hits Keith Fletcher on his England cap, 1974–75

Thomson also specialised in finding lift off a length. Amiss referred to his 'trapdoor ball' – so called because it came out of nowhere. The same thing could have been said of the man himself. Thomson was 24 when he faced England, a bleached-blond beach bum who seemed to have washed in with the tide. There was a sense of mystery about him that made him all the more frightening. In those first few weeks, his potency seemed limitless.

Thomson's catalogue of terrors would eventually bring him 200 Test wickets, yet he never bowled faster than he did against England in 1974–75. His part in the series ended during the fifth Test at Adelaide, when he ripped shoulder muscles playing tennis on the rest day. But even after a number of debilitating injuries, he still clocked 99.7mph at a televised time trial four years later, fully 10mph ahead of Michael Holding and Imran Khan.

According to Alan Knott, the England wicketkeeper: 'I thought for four Tests he was a genius. After that he never bowled the same and was never as hostile. It was a tragedy he got injured.' Not according to a generation of opening batsmen, it wasn't.

DIFFERENT STROKES

How should a batsman go about facing up to what *Wisden* called 'the greatest battering in the history of the game'? England's approaches varied. There was Edrich, the human punchbag. There was Denness, who backed away to square-leg and invariably ended up flashing the ball into the slips. And then there was Tony Greig, who behaved as if the whole tour was a test of his masculinity.

'Fetch that!'

England's South African-born all-rounder Tony Greig yells at Australian fast bowler Dennis Lillee after hitting him for a boundary, Brisbane, 1974–75

When Australia batted first at Brisbane, Lillee's arrival at the crease prompted England's opening bowlers, Willis and Peter Lever, to lay off the short stuff. No one really knew how quickly Lillee might bowl after his long lay-off, but there seemed little point in prodding a hornet's nest, just on the off chance that it might be unoccupied. Greig disagreed. Asking for the ball, he hurled down a succession of bouncers at Lillee, soon having him caught behind as he fended another short ball off his face. An incensed Lillee stormed back to the dressing-room, slammed his bat into his locker and announced 'Just remember who started this – those bastards. But we'll finish it.'

When Greig's turn came to bat, Lillee gave him a bouncer first ball. No surprises there. He then walked down the pitch, fixing Greig with his best psychopathic stare, and made a mark on his own forehead with his finger. For the next five hours, the pair were locked in one of the most riveting battles in Ashes history. When Lillee pitched short of a length, Greig would uppercut him over the slips, before going down on one knee, signalling a boundary, and yelling 'Fetch that!' When Lillee bowled a genuine bouncer, Greig pretended to head the ball away. This almost hysterical performance was designed to prove to Lillee – and perhaps to himself – that he wasn't intimidated. The result was a magnificent 110, the only century scored by an Englishman until Thomson's injury.

Greig's flamboyance was in marked contrast to the desperate crease occupation practised by most of his team-mates. Another man who preferred to soak up the punishment was Edrich's

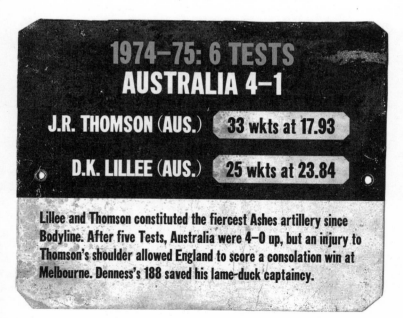

1974–75: 6 TESTS
AUSTRALIA 4–1

J.R. THOMSON (AUS.)   33 wkts at 17.93

D.K. LILLEE (AUS.)   25 wkts at 23.84

Lillee and Thomson constituted the fiercest Ashes artillery since Bodyline. After five Tests, Australia were 4–0 up, but an injury to Thomson's shoulder allowed England to score a consolation win at Melbourne. Denness's 188 saved his lame-duck captaincy.

injury replacement, Colin Cowdrey. Now 41, Cowdrey was flown out from snowbound Kent just in time for the Perth Test. When told of the call-up, Thomson remarked bluntly: 'He'll cop it too.'

According to Greig, the first the players saw of Cowdrey was when he alighted from a taxi, 'dressed in a typical City of London pin-striped business suit and with . . . a particularly pale complexion. I shall never forget Max Walker's reaction: "Thommo and Lillee will kill him stone dead!"'

In fact, Cowdrey played the gruesome twosome better than most. He endured for more than two hours in both innings, which was a tribute to his bulldog spirit. He also effected cricket's most famous introduction when he went up to Thomson at a drinks break, stuck out his hand, and said: 'How do you do, I'm Colin Cowdrey.'

Thomson had already landed some fearsome blows on Cowdrey's pear-shaped figure, but he shook the proffered hand politely and replied: 'G'day, I'm Jeff Thomson.' It was what Cowdrey described as 'a Livingstone and Stanley moment'. A moment or two later, the barrage started all over again.

'Yeah, I'd drink with 'em. Trouble is, you can never find any Poms to drink with, can you Dennis?'

Jeff Thomson offers the Poms a tinnie, 1974–75

DIFFERENT FOLKS

Poor old Denness. His experience of Ashes cricket was nasty, brutish and short. After just one Test of the 1975 series he left the stage for good, probably cursing the fact that a quirk of the fixture list had brought him up against that vicious harridan Lillian Thomson twice in the space of six months.

The selectors' choice of replacement might have shocked a few. Tony Greig was the first England captain to also be a Woozer (White Urban English-Speaking South African). But despite his origins on the Eastern Cape, Greig became a great favourite of buttoned-up Englishmen like the *Daily Telegraph*'s Jim Swanton. *Wisden*, showing a questionable grasp of geography, described him as 'the Nordic superman made flesh'.

Greig did not actually win a Test in 1975, but three draws represented a substantial advance on Denness. He also came up with arguably the most inspired selectorial bolter of them all: David Steele for England.

This one really did come out of the blue. Steele had spent 12 undistinguished years with Northamptonshire before his call-up, which sent him straight into the teeth of Australia's predatory attack. Or it would have sent him straight there, if he hadn't gone down one too many flights of stairs in the Lord's pavilion and found himself in the gents' toilets. It was the first surprise of a summer in which Steele endeared himself to the British public. Steele looked less like a professional cricketer than an amateur enthusiast, the kind of man who turns out every weekend for Little Frottage in the Village Blacksmith League. At 33, he wore

> **'Who's this, then? Father f***ing Christmas?'**
>
> Jeff Thomson greets the silver-haired David Steele, Lord's, 1975

'That Randall! He bats like an octopus with piles.'
Spectator to *Wisden* editor Matthew Engel, Adelaide

David 'Stainless' Steele, first-choice batsman for the England over-achievers' XI: he scored 50 and 45 on debut at Lord's after losing his way from the home dressing-room to the wicket and ending up in the gents' toilets

steel-rimmed glasses and had prematurely silver hair. In *The Sun*, Clive Taylor memorably described him as 'the bank clerk who went to war'. Even Thomson raised an eyebrow when this unlikely figure emerged from the Long Room. 'Who's this then?' he quipped. 'Father 'f***ing Christmas?'

Once 'Stainless' had finally navigated his way to the crease, the Australians did not find it easy to wipe him away. He batted for almost 19 hours in the series, for a lowest score of 39 and a high of 92. Not even the appearance of English cricket's first streaker could break his phenomenal concentration.

When Steele fell just short of his hundred at Headingley, John Snow wrote: 'I think the whole country felt for him . . . Even the Australians did, and they don't give anything away.' But Steele went one better: in December, he became the first cricketer to win BBC Sports Personality of the Year since Jim Laker. At the start of the season, you could have got shorter odds on Benny Hill eloping with Germaine Greer.

Orthodox batsmen rarely succeeded against Lillee and Thomson, but it seemed the more idiosyncratic you were, the more chance you had. Derek Randall walked out to bat for the 1977 Centenary Test in Melbourne singing 'The Sun Has Got His Hat On, Hip-Hip-Hip-Hooray.' His antics over the next seven hours

1975: 4 TESTS
AUSTRALIA 1–0

D.K. LILLEE (AUS.) | 21 wkts at 21.90

D.S. STEELE (ENG.) | 365 runs at 60.83

This series was shortened to make room for the inaugural World Cup. Lillee and Thomson rolled England again at Edgbaston, but the advent of Tony Greig as captain and David Steele in the top order stemmed the bleeding. The third Test had to be abandoned after supporters of the armed robber George Davis dug up the pitch.

made Greig look like an introvert. He doffed his cap to Lillee's bouncers, or bowed, or rolled onto his back. When one finally caught up with him, striking him a glancing blow on the head, he remarked: 'No good hitting me there mate, nothing to damage.'

During another Randall hundred in 1982–83, an exasperated Lillee was moved to remark: 'I hate bowling at you. I'm not as good at hitting a moving target.'

Randall was a genuine English eccentric, and never more so than in his own house. His wife Liz once confessed that: 'When we were first married, Derek used to throw tea cups behind his back and catch them. That's one way he got out of doing the washing-up.' Ian Botham visited Randall in the late 1970s, and was surprised to find her 'answering the door bell wearing a pretty dress and a set of pads'. Inside, Randall was lounging around in a matching pair. 'Just breaking my gear in for the new season,' he exclaimed cheerfully.

'When are your balls going to drop, sonny?' 'I don't know, but at least I'm playing cricket for my own country.'

Exchange between South African-born England captain Tony Greig and the young David Hookes, Centenary Test, Melbourne, 1977

THE REVOLUTION WILL BE TELEVISED

Greig took on the captaincy with those Nordic
eyes wide open. 'I'd got it from a guy who'd
thought he was going to hang on to it for a
long time,' he recalled. 'Who'd got it in turn
from someone who thought he was going to
hang on to it for a long time . . . I knew a tenure
could be ended by one bad report, one incident,
one bit of foul language.'

Determined to beat the bastards to the punch, Greig spent just
two years in the job before staging the most dramatic exit by
any international captain (with the possible exception of South
Africa's match-fixer Hansie Cronje). He was the first England
cricketer to sign for Kerry Packer, a bumptious Australian
broadcaster with plans for a breakaway circuit. In doing so, he
became a pariah, sacked by the England selectors and booed by
county crowds. 'Jeez, he was like Lord Haw-Haw,' remarked
the Australian batsman Ross Edwards. 'He was very bad meat.'

Packer's intervention was a seminal moment for cricket.
Before he came along, his jacket pocket bulging with lucrative
contracts, administrators around the world had treated their
players like skivvies. The Australian board were particularly
high-handed. On Bill Lawry's tour of India in 1969–70, the
team had been billeted in a string of unsanitary hovels. Yet if

**'The count for the first season was 13 "shits",
14 "you bastards", three "f***s" and one "c***".'**
World Series Cricket director John Crilly on profanities picked up
by pitch microphones in WSC's first season

the players complained, the response was always the same:
'If they don't like the conditions there are 500,000 other
cricketers in Australia who would love to take their places.'

All Packer really wanted was a fair chance to bid against the
Australian Broadcasting Corporation for Test coverage. Faced
with a recalcitrant cricket board in Melbourne, his heavy-handed
approach – 'Come on gentlemen, there is a little bit of the whore
in all of us when it comes to money' – must count as one of the
most ill-conceived chat-up lines in history.

Packer then flew to London, where he received a similar
rebuff from the English authorities. His response was to press the
red button on his time bomb. 'It's every man for himself,' he
stormed, 'and the devil take the hindmost.'

At the height of the controversy, the establishment threatened
to ban any player who signed for Packer. Greig responded with
a restraint of trade suit. 'For some reason I felt like a criminal,'
he admitted, after his interrogation in London's High Court. But
Justice Slade found in Greig's favour: the bans were unlawful,
and Packer was free to start packing them in.

Kerry Packer's World Series Cricket (WSC) was what
happened when cricket shared a bed with capitalism. Its
provocative slogan, 'Big Boys Play At Night', heralded the
introduction of floodlights, white balls, coloured pyjamas and
drop-in pitches – all ideas that are still in use today. The
broadcasters experimented with pitch microphones, occasionally
taking the viewer closer to the action than anyone had intended.
'The count for the first season was something like 13 "shits", 14
"you bastards", three "f***s" and one "c***" that got on the air,'
according to director John Crilly. 'We were still learning and a
few people were a bit slow with the faders.'

'The most dangerous act in the entertainment business these days is not balancing on a high wire or even putting a head in a lion's mouth. It is batting in Kerry Packer's Flying Circus. Fast bowling and repeated bouncers are destroying some of the best batsmen we have ever seen.'

Former England captain Tony Lewis

Tony Greig prepares for World Series Cricket, which he secretly helped Kerry Packer to set up in 1977. 'There's only one head bigger than Tony Greig's – and that's Birkenhead,' said Fred Trueman

Many of those expletives were supplied by batsmen limbo-dancing under a succession of life-threatening bouncers. WSC did not just possess a golden generation of fast bowlers; it also had a macho culture, encouraged by bloodthirsty TV executives and *laissez-faire* umpires.

The former England captain Tony Lewis wrote: 'The most dangerous act in the entertainment business these days is not balancing on a high wire or even putting a head in a lion's mouth. It is batting in Kerry Packer's Flying Circus. Fast bowling and repeated bouncers are destroying some of the best batsmen we have ever seen.'

The prospect of facing a global array of speed freaks like the West Indies' Andy Roberts and Pakistan's Imran Khan on sporting pitches was enough to set anyone thinking. And these were not pretty thoughts. If you were to miss a hook shot, the next thing in the back of your mind could be the front of your mind. When Roberts felled Australia's golden boy David Hookes with his dreaded one-two combination – slow, sit-up-and-hit-me bouncer, followed by shorter, faster killer ball – the embryonic helmet industry exploded almost as dramatically as Hookes's jawbone.

> **'His ability to be where fast bowlers aren't has long been a talking point among cricketers.'**
> **Tony Greig questions Geoff Boycott's** *cojones*

Over WSC's two trailblazing summers, most of the world's finest cricketers traded blows. But not everyone came to play. Greig could not resist a jibe at his absent adversary Geoff Boycott, who had testified against him in the High Court. 'His ability to be where fast bowlers aren't has long been a talking point among cricketers,' Greig sneered.

LAMBS TO THE SLAUGHTER

The munificence of World Series might have ensured cricketers a fair wage, but it did nothing for Australia's Ashes prospects. Greg Chappell's 1977 tourists to England are remembered as the team that Packer poisoned.

Around two-thirds of the Australian squad had signed before they even boarded the plane, under an oath of absolute secrecy. No one knew whether their best mates were in or out until the story broke in the papers a week later. The dressing-room split left younger players like 23-year-old Kim Hughes feeling bewildered and betrayed. Politics were inescapable on that tour, though Chappell and his clique did their best. According to another new boy, Gary Cosier, 'It got to the stage where you only saw the senior players on the field.'

Packer also insisted on access to his men at any time, however inconvenient. The director John Crilly spent the rest day of the second Test recording interviews, with the help of a bucket of booze to loosen the players' tongues. When Australia went down by nine wickets, Crilly wondered whether he, rather than Derek Underwood, should have been England's man of the match.

> **'Jeez, it's not even as cold as this in my fridge back in Brisbane.'**
> Jeff Thomson on the early-season English weather

By the time Brearley's Englishmen made their return visit, 18 months later, World Series Cricket was forging ahead of the established format. Packer had bought up not one but two full XIs of Australia's best players. The first team faced opposition from

the West Indies and the Rest of the
World in the awe-inspiring SuperTests
– arguably the most furiously
competitive matches ever staged. The
second-string players mooched around
small-town venues in the Country Cup. If life in the sticks began to
drag, they could always pass the time by stacking up their money.

The 1978–79 Ashes were relegated to the status of a sideshow
– or should that be freakshow? The sight of Australia going down
5–1 to the Poms was certainly hard to credit, though precious few
people actually witnessed it. 'It wasn't our fault the crowds stayed
away,' wrote England's emerging star David Gower. 'Are we to
blame because the Aussies don't like a losing side?'

In the general confusion, Australia seemed to be playing
everyone out of position. The captain, Graham Yallop, was a
painfully introverted 26-year-old with just eight Tests to his name.
Nos 2 and 3 in the batting line-up were filled by Gary Cosier

1977: 5 TESTS
ENGLAND 3–0

G. BOYCOTT (ENG.) — 442 runs at 147.33

R.G.D. WILLIS (ENG.) — 27 wkts at 19.77

A rare chance for England to grind down a divided and dispirited
Australian squad. Two-thirds of the touring players had signed up
with Kerry Packer before even boarding the plane. Recalled for
the third Test, Boycott notched his 98th first-class century, then
added his 100th on his home ground of Headingley.

1978–79: 6 TESTS
ENGLAND 5–1

I.T. BOTHAM (ENG.) — 23 wkts at 24.65 & 291 runs at 29.10

R.M. HOGG (AUS.) — 41 wkts at 12.85

Hogg's haul could not stop England running away with the series. Yallop's third-string Australia briefly threatened to level at 2–2, after taking a 142-run lead in the fourth Test, but Derek Randall's 10-hour 150 closed the door on them.

Been there, won the Ashes, bought the T-shirt. The clothes and hairstyles of the mid-1970s as exemplified by England's Geoff Miller, John Lever, Bob Willis, Graham Roope and Derek Randall, The Oval, August 1977

and Peter Toohey, a pair of middle-order cavaliers. The bowling attack, based around the unheralded trio of Hogg, Higgs and Hurst, sounded as if it had been picked by a selector with hiccups.

In fact, Rodney Hogg turned out to be Australia's one success story. He was quick enough to regularly burst through Boycott's defences, and nasty enough to come up to Gower after a flukey century at Perth and snarl: 'F***ing impostor.' But in this summer of rifts, Yallop could not even keep his best bowler onside. The pair of them had a red-faced row on the Adelaide outfield, after Yallop objected to Hogg's regular rest-stops. 'At one stage Hogg suggested we survey the back of the Adelaide Oval,' Yallop wrote, 'and I don't think he had a tennis match on his mind.'

In his account of the tour, *Lambs To The Slaughter*, Yallop is even-handed in apportioning the blame. Everyone cops it: the selectors, the media, even the groundsmen. The only man he doesn't accuse is the one who was ultimately responsible – Kerry Packer himself. Perhaps he realised he would never have been writing a book in the first place without Packer's inadvertent help.

A month or two later, the whole saga was over. In May 1979, the Australian board granted Packer exclusive rights to their home internationals, including a triangular, floodlit, pyjama-clad one-day tournament to be known as the World Series Cup. They were also canny enough to sign him up as their marketing agent and promoter. The men in suits had discovered their inner whore.

A GREAT ASHES ROMANCE

Ian Botham needed only a few hours of Test cricket to establish his ascendancy over Australia's batsmen. At Trent Bridge in 1977, Botham took five for 74, opening his account in typically golden-armed style when Greg Chappell chopped a wide long-hop onto his stumps.

It was the beginning of a beautiful romance. Botham loved playing against the Aussies, and the Aussies respected and admired him in return. There was something mystical about his hold on the Australian psyche. Even when his back had gone, and his figure had become more Porky than Beefy, watching him bowl at the old enemy was still like watching Dr Who outwitting a legion of Daleks, armed only with a sonic screwdriver.

After close of play, Botham spent plenty of time larking about with larrikins like Marsh and Lillee. Instinctive, irreverent and insubordinate, Botham had all the qualities Australians most valued in a cricketer. If he had been born in Cairns rather than Cheshire, those long years of Baggy Green domination would have started a good deal earlier.

The one Australian who never warmed to Botham's earthy charms was Ian Chappell. The explanation may lie in an argument in the bar of the Melbourne Cricket Ground, some time in early 1977. The details of the story are disputed. Each man claims that the other was mouthing off in a drunken and offensive way, but the one thing they both agree on is that Botham punched or pushed Chappell backwards off his stool. Botham then says that he pursued the fleeing Chappell out of the door, 'hurdling

Ian Botham enjoys a dressing-room cigar after his 149 not out at Headingley, 20 July 1981. Fast bowler Bob Willis applied the *coup de grâce* the following day

'The Indians used to call him "Iron Bottom", but he wasn't – not after all that f***in' curry.'

John Emburey, speaking of Botham after a tour of India

the bonnet of a car in the chase'; Chappell's story is that Botham threatened to cut him from ear to ear with a broken bottle.

Three decades later, you might imagine that the aftershocks of this beery fracas would have died down. Far from it. When the pair of them recently found themselves commentating on the same match, the interviewer Ray Martin asked Chappell: 'You'll be having a drink with him after the commentary is over?' The reply was: 'No, Ray. I can find plenty of decent people to have a drink with.'

Botham was still a relative nobody when he squared up to Chappell in the MCG bar. But by the time they met on the field, in 1979–80, he was a much bigger noise. Over those first couple of years of his career, Botham had everything going for him: waspish swing in either direction, a procession of denuded, Packerised teams to lord it over, and an avuncular captain in Mike Brearley. After 25 Tests, Botham's vital statistics (batting average 40.48, bowling average 18.52) classed him as the finest cricketer ever to wear a mullet.

Then came the first of many abrupt U-turns. Brearley gave up the captaincy to concentrate on his training as a psychoanalyist. Botham took over, and soon felt like he needed a shrink himself. It was not just the results that got him down, though he failed to win a single one of his 12 Tests in charge. It was also the fact that he failed to register a single century or five-wicket haul. The golden arm had lost its golden touch.

Botham was unfortunate, in that his reign began with back-to-back series against the West Indies. Shades of Denness here, as Clive Lloyd's side were then the strongest in the game. He may also have been a casualty of the Peter Principle, which states that people inevitably rise beyond their sphere of excellence. As Bob Willis put it: 'Botham was just one of those people who was a natural cricketer. And that sort of cricketer doesn't have to think too deeply about the game.'

G.S. CHAPPELL (AUS.) 317 runs at 79.25

D.K. LILLEE (AUS.) 23 wkts at 16.87

Try telling the Australians that the Ashes were not up for grabs in this short series. Despite all-round heroics by Botham (19 wkts at 19.53, including 11 for 176 at Perth, and 119 not out at Melbourne), Greg Chappell's back-to-full-strength Australia gave England a vengeful stuffing.

Brearley addressed the same issue in his classic book *The Art of Captaincy*, albeit in slightly different language: 'I recall Tacitus's cautionary mot about the Emperor Galba, that he was *capax imperii nisi imperasset* – capable of ruling, if he had not ruled.' If only Brearley's batting had been so classical.

However you conjugated it, Botham's reign was a disaster, and he eventually resigned an hour after the second Test of the 1981 Ashes. The last straw was the reaction to his first-ball duck in that game. 'Not a soul among the Lord's members mumbled "bad luck", and not a single MCC member looked me in the eye,' he wrote. 'From that day on I never raised a bat to acknowledge them at Lord's.'

THE MIRACLE OF HEADINGLEY

A year's worth of frustration had been building up inside Botham. And in the next game, the dam burst in spectacular fashion. This was arguably the most famous of all Ashes Tests. So famous, in fact, that the Headingley miracle became a millstone for English cricket.

'Come on, let's give it some humpty.'

Ian Botham unleashes hell, Headingley, 1981

The theory goes that Botham's heroics had a corrosive effect on the team ethic. Not only did he promote the cult of the individual, but the way he prepared for matches – often by downing five pints and a curry – gave the impression that inspiration could be turned on like a tap. Certainly England underachieved throughout the 1980s, despite Botham's presence and that of other talents like Gower, Gatting and Lamb. The only side they could be relied on to beat was Australia.

The story of Headingley began with the reappointment of Brearley. His first move was to go up to his prime all-rounder and ask: 'Beef, are you sure you want to play? If you don't, I will fully understand.' When Botham replied 'Of course,' Brearley told him: 'That's great. I think you'll get 150 runs and take 10 wickets.'

Things looked grim at the halfway stage. England, already one down in the series, were bowled out for 174 and asked to follow on. Up to that point, the only positive had been Botham, who took six for 95, struck 50 from 54 balls, and could be seen laughing and joking with Lillee in his old manner. 'Botham's change of mood was obvious to everybody,' Graham Dilley would comment.

1981: 6 TESTS
ENGLAND 3–1

I.T. BOTHAM (ENG.) — 34 wkts at 20.58 & 399 runs at 36.27

T.M. ALDERMAN (AUS.) — 42 wkts at 21.26

Relieved of the captaincy after two ineffectual Tests, Botham's unforgettable sequence began with 199 runs and seven wickets in England's epic win at Headingley. He then took five for 11 to ambush Australia again at Edgbaston, and blazed a stupendous 118 – containing six sixes and taking up just 102 balls – at Old Trafford.

'It was almost as if you'd taken a child, made him an adult for a while, then allowed him to go back to being a child.'

As England came off for bad light, early in their second innings, the electronic scoreboard flashed up the Ladbrokes prices: England 500–1, Australia 1–4. They were daft odds for a two-horse race, but Ladbrokes thought they had spotted a chance to get some cheap publicity. After all, no team had won a Test after following on since the 19th century (see page 34).

Lillee and Rod Marsh broke every rule in the book when they sent their bus driver to place £10 and £5 respectively on an England win. They had originally wanted to stake £50 of the team fund, but were shouted down by their team-mates. England's wicketkeeper Bob Taylor had also wanted to stake £20 but ran into a crowd of young autograph-hunters and had to abandon the chase.

While the bet became a controversial issue after the game, no one with any sense has ever accused this pair of Ockers of deliberately throwing a match. 'Marsh and Lillee would have a punt on the Martians landing if they had got those odds,' said David Gower. 'They've had a few bets on horses that barely answered to the description.'

Both teams spent Saturday night at a boozy barbecue at Botham's place in Lincolnshire and, when the game resumed on Monday, England's procession continued. They were 135 for seven, still 92 behind, when Dilley joined Botham at the crease. 'You don't fancy hanging around on this wicket for a day and a half, do you?' Dilley did not. 'Come on,' Botham replied, 'let's give it some humpty.'

> **'Don't even bother looking for that one. It's gone straight into the confectionery stall – and out again.'**
>
> Richie Benaud greets a Botham straight six, Headingley, 1981

The result was a maiden Test fifty for Dilley and a barrage of boundaries for Botham, who smashed the ball everywhere in what Yallop called 'an educated slog'. Even his mishits – and there were a fair few of those – were nearly going for six. His eventual total was 149 not out from 148 balls, with 27 fours and a straight six that gave rise to a Richie Benaud classic: 'Don't even bother looking for that one. It's gone straight into the confectionery stall – and out again.' England were finally bowled out on the fifth morning for 356, 129 runs ahead.

'Ian just wanted to entertain the crowd,' Willis said. 'It was inside edge, outside edge, over the keeper, wide of the keeper. Later on it was a dramatic piece of batting, but I still think if Kim Hughes had brought on Ray Bright, the spinner, they'd have won. Ian would have hit one up in the air, but by the time they turned to spin he had his eye in and you couldn't set a field because the ground wasn't big enough.'

The final act belonged to Willis himself. Beset by illness and knee trouble, his place had been in doubt, and he only just made this team ahead of John Emburey. But he found an unstoppable rhythm downhill from the Kirkstall Lane End, with the wind at his back. His

Bob Willis is mobbed after England's astounding 18-run victory at Headingley, 1981. 'I looked into his eyes and it was like there was nobody there,' said Graham Dilley

figures of eight for 43, bowling Australia out for 111 and clinching the match by 18 runs, were won through sheer pace, hostility, and – according to his team-mates – a bizarre trancelike state. 'I looked into his eyes and it was like there was nobody there,' said Dilley.

The truth of this can still be judged by Patrick Eagar's great photograph of the team running off the field. Gatting, Gooch and Willey are all beaming from ear to ear – or rather from whisker to whisker. And then there is Willis, clean-shaven and bug-eyed, looking like an extra from *Dawn of the Dead*.

NOTORIOUSER AND NOTORIOUSER

According to Len Hutton, Botham was 'the first rock-and-roll cricketer'. This was an accurate judgement as far as it went, but whatever happened to the sex and drugs, let alone the violence?

When Botham was not emptying bars, he was draining them dry with his coterie of celebrity drinking chums – Elton, Eric and Ringo among them. Once play was over, the best sight his team-mates got of him was in the pages of the tabloids, which were then entering their vicious heyday.

In a classic case of double-think, *The Sun* paid Botham for a column while simultaneously printing huge headlines about his brawls, drug scandals and supposed affairs. The relationship limped on until 1988, when Botham spent a night in a Perth lock-up after allegedly assaulting a passenger on an internal Australian flight. When the paper rang, asking for a first-person piece, he finally pulled the plug.

Whether as author or subject, Botham made good copy. In 1982–83, the Australian public were fascinated by the saga of the piglet smuggled into the Gabba by a group of veterinary students. Released onto the outfield, the confused animal had 'Botham' written on one side and 'Eddie' (Hemmings) on the other, in reference to the generous proportions of England's two most corpulent bowlers. For a week afterwards, the Australian papers were full of appeals for a family who would give the pig a home.

The next Ashes year, 1985, started with a real Botham special. On New Year's Day, the story

'If you've signed the c*, you can sack the c***.'**
Kelvin MacKenzie, mild-mannered editor of *The Sun*, after Botham's resignation as captain, 1981

> **'This fellow is the most overrated player I have ever seen. He looks too heavy, and the way he's been bowling out here, he wouldn't burst a paper bag.'**
> Former England fast-bowling great Harold Larwood
> is underwhelmed by Botham, 1983

A confused piglet roams the outfield at the Gabba, the names 'Botham' and 'Eddie' scrawled on its flanks, 1982–83. The animal was smuggled into the ground with an apple in its mouth. As far as the security guard was concerned, it was on its way to the barbie

broke that the Humberside police had found 2.19 grammes of cannabis at his house the previous night. Yet Lord's seemed more concerned about Botham's penchant for another illegal substance: the reverse-sweep. When he got out that way during a one-day international, a po-faced Peter May (now England's chairman of selectors) told reporters: 'I have thumbed through the MCC coaching manual and found that no such stroke exists.'

The summer of 1985 was actually one of the wettest in living memory, but in the mind's eye, the sun was always shining on Gower's curly blond locks as he laced another languid boundary through the covers. Botham had dyed his mullet blond in sympathy, and he came out with the intention of bowling as fast as he could and hitting everything for six. In the fifth Test, he rifled his first ball back over the head of a bemused Craig McDermott into the Edgbaston pavilion.

David Gower in his great summer of 1985. As Tanya Aldred wrote: 'Even now, I can recite the litany of results for that series. A sort of: divorced, beheaded, died, divorced, beheaded, survived – but more memorable'

Just when it seemed Botham's ego could not get any bigger, he ran into Tim Hudson, a Walter Mitty-ish agent who promised to make him a Hollywood star. In early 1986, Hudson plonked his man on a plane to meet the producer Monachem Golan. The idea was that Golan was going to turn Botham into the next 007, but the closest he got was a photo opportunity in the Wild West section of the Universal Studios' public tour.

In *Botham: My Autobiography*, Hudson is described as being 'away with the fairies'. He was sacked the following year, after telling a group of reporters. 'I'm aware [Botham] smokes dope. Doesn't everybody?' Yet Botham – or at least his ghost-writer – could not resist reproducing one long passage from Hudson's (unpublished) diaries.

When Botham is around women, Hudson wrote, he 'becomes like a Roman gladiator at the feast of something or other. Women find it more than difficult not to cross and uncross their legs under his gaze. They seem to breathe much quicker and their chests begin to heave as the nipples push against the soft T-shirt fabric or the silk blouses. He's definitely every woman's piece of rough . . . in the long, long grass . . . by the lake . . . under a full moon.'

'Blimey, Beefy, who writes your scripts?'
Graham Gooch to Ian Botham after he dismisses New Zealand's Bruce Edgar with his first ball after a two-month drugs ban, 1986

1982–83: 5 TESTS
AUSTRALIA 2–1

K.J. HUGHES (AUS.) | 469 runs at 67.00

G.F. LAWSON (AUS.) | 34 wkts at 20.20

It was England's turn to be weakened, thanks to Gooch's rebel tour of South Africa. At Melbourne, the tourists brought the score back to 2–1 with a thrilling three-run win against the run of play. But a century from Kim Hughes made the final Test (and the Ashes) safe for Australia.

1985: 6 TESTS
ENGLAND 3–1

I.T. BOTHAM (ENG.) | 31 wkts at 27.58 & 250 runs at 31.25

D.I. GOWER (ENG.) | 732 runs at 81.33

The series was poised at 1–1 after four Tests, but England won both the last two games comfortably. The key was the call-up of Richard Ellison, an unlikely hero with a white man's Afro. Hooping the ball round corners, Ellison took ten wickets at Birmingham and seven at The Oval, where Gooch and Gower shared a 351-run stand.

BEEFY'S LAST BOW

From the 1970s on, it has become almost traditional that the first question asked to every England captain at an Australian airport should be: 'So Mike/Bob/Graham, this must be the worst English team ever to reach these shores?' In 1986–87, it seemed that the questioners had a point.

England, now captained by Mike Gatting, were coming off a shocking sequence: no Test wins and eight defeats since the last Ashes series in 1985. The streak showed no sign of ending as a side full of novices limped through their early tour matches, losing to Queensland and very nearly to Western Australia. After a broadside from *The Independent*'s cricket correspondent, Warwickshire fast bowler Gladstone Small recalls: 'We became the team of can'ts: can't bat, can't bowl, can't field.'

Still, there was always Botham. At England's eve-of-series dinner, the big man stood up and gave a pep-talk. 'His point was that anything that had happened in the warm-ups was irrelevant,' said Gatting. 'From now on it was just 11 men against 11. It was quite a reasoned speech for Beefy. Normally his strategy didn't go much beyond: "I'll bounce him out, then I'll bounce him out, then I'll knock his block off."'

Not always the most reliable role model, Botham proceeded to smash a spectacular 138 the next day, so setting the tone for one of England's most rewarding

> **'We became the team of can'ts: can't bat, can't bowl, can't field.'**
>
> Fast bowler Gladstone Small on England's 1986–87 Ashes team

'At least I have an identity. You're only Frances Edmonds's husband.'
Australian wicketkeeper Tim Zoehrer responds to sledging by England's slow left-armer Phil Edmonds

Ashes tours. They won everything going that winter, not only the Test series but also two one-day trophies.

Australians turned the usual blind eye to England's retention of the Ashes at Melbourne, preferring to focus on tennis star Pat Cash and his Davis Cup triumph. But this was still an intriguing match, culminating in a sledging battle between England's slow left-armer Phil Edmonds and Australia's wicketkeeper Tim Zoehrer. After a few obscenities from Edmonds at short-leg, Zoehrer came out with the smart retort: 'At least I have an identity. You're only Frances Edmonds's husband.'

Frances Edmonds was the author of a best-selling account of the previous winter's trip to the West Indies (*Another Bloody Tour*), but Phil had literary aspirations too. At the close of play, he went into the Australian dressing-room to deliver a limerick: 'There was a young glove-man named Zoehrer / Whose keeping got poorer and poorer / Said AB from first slip / "Please stop giving lip / And with extras stop troubling the scorer."' (AB was Allan Border.)

Zoehrer, not to be outdone, started composing his response: 'There was a balding old man called Philippe / Who stands in the gully too deep / When his turn came to bat / He opened his trap / And his innings just fell in a heap.'

Neither was Botham quite done with the Aussies yet. A portly figure during the 1992 World Cup, he still annihilated Allan Border's side one last time, with four wickets and a half-century. Three weeks later,

'I dunno. Maybe it's that tally-ho lads attitude. You know, there'll always be an England, all that Empire crap they dish out. But I never could cop Poms.'
Jeff Thomson has one last pop at the Poms, 1987

Rocket man, cricket fan: Phil Edmonds (foreground) and Phil DeFreitas celebrate England's 1986–87 series victory with Elton John

he was back in the headlines for walking out on a comedian who had been lampooning the Queen. When Paul Keating described Botham's reaction as 'precious', he replied: 'I'm very, very proud of my heritage – and, unlike Mr Keating, I have one.'

It was fitting that Botham should have made his final first-class appearance against the 1993 Australians. The mood was captured by his Durham team-mate Simon Hughes. 'As Botham sent down an assortment of phantom seamers and slow bouncers to the Australian openers, the rest of the team looked on, mesmerised. Steve Waugh, the next man in, was on tenterhooks, the others

'I'm very, very proud of my heritage – and, unlike Mr Keating, I have one.'
Ian Botham on Australian prime minister Paul Keating, 1992

watched in reverence. "Cor blimey!" Allan Border exclaimed. "What's he tried now?" Merv Hughes asked, preferring not to watch. "One that Boony couldn't reach!" Shane Warne said. "He'll snaffle him in a minute, you bet," Hughes predicted.'

It was an exercise in mystique over matter, but this time even Botham could not blag himself a wicket. At the age of 37, he was taking five minutes just to get out of bed in the morning. And now that the Australians had got his measure, he knew it was time to give the game away.

1986–87: 5 TESTS
ENGLAND 2–1

B.C. BROAD (ENG.) 487 runs at 69.57

D.M. JONES (AUS.) 511 runs at 56.77

Botham scored one hundred and took one five-for in this series, and both turned out to be match-winners. Gatting, the England captain, was still furious when his side collapsed to unheralded off-spinner Peter Taylor in the final match, handing Australia their first win in 15 Tests. Taylor's selection was widely believed to be an accident, resulting from confusion with his namesake Mark Taylor.

THE BAGGY GREEN MACHINE

1989—PRESENT

CAPTAIN AUSTRALIA

Almost two decades after Ian Chappell reinvented Australian cricket, Allan Border did it all over again. Border's 1989 tourists epitomised the gum-chewing Baggy Green machine. In one summer of bristling moustaches and gimlet eyes, they razed English cricket so thoroughly that the green shoots took an awfully long time to appear.

This was the year when buses all over London were carrying the slogan 'Australians wouldn't give a XXXX for anything else'. Border certainly didn't give a XXXX for etiquette. He banned the traditional post-match pint with the opposition, telling his opposite number David Gower, 'The last time I came here, I was a nice guy who came last.' Only once the Ashes had been secured did he lift the ban, accepting Gower's dinner invitation and explaining: 'I've been through all sorts of downs with my team but this time I thought we had a bloody good chance to win and I was prepared to be as ruthless as it takes to stuff you. I didn't mind upsetting anyone, my own team-mates included, as long as we got the right result.'

The new-look Border was about as touchy-feely as a steel hawser. His captaincy mirrored his batting: limited at first, but redeemed by limitless grit. The Australian wicketkeeper Wally Grout once said of Ken

> **'What do you think this is, a f***ing tea party? No, you can't have a f***ing glass of water. You can f***ing wait like the rest of us.'**
> **Allan Border to Robin Smith, Trent Bridge, 1989**

**Border the brooder: after playing in five Ashes series and winning
just once, Allan Border resolved to stick it up the Poms**

Barrington that: 'Whenever Ken walked to the wicket I thought
a Union Jack was trailing behind him.' The same line would apply
to Border, only with the Southern Cross.

While Brearley made great play of treating his men as
individuals, Border preferred to mould a team in his own
tenacious image. Perhaps the defining moment of his captaincy
came in September 1986, during the tied Test against India in
Madras. Dean Jones was dizzy and sick with dehydration, in the
middle of his epic 210, and as he tells it: 'I mentioned to AB that

> ## 'The mincing run-up resembles someone in high heels and a panty girdle chasing after a bus.'
> ### Merv Hughes, as seen by cricket writer Martin Johnson

I had had enough, and . . . his reply was quick: "Let's get a tough Australian out here then, if you can't handle it any more. Let's get a Queenslander! Greg Ritchie can handle this!" So I told him what he could do with his tough bloody Queenslander, and batted on.' Jones's reward – apart from a night on a saline drip in hospital – was the respect and loyalty of his captain.

Border had his Lillee substitute in Merv Hughes, a caricature of the huge and hairy antipodean fast bowler. There was an element of absurdity about Hughes's mincing run-up, described by one cricket writer as resembling 'someone in high heels and a panty girdle chasing after a bus'. But there were few batsmen laughing at Hughes, at least not within his earshot. He had unerring accuracy, a heat-seeking bouncer, and a heart as big as Shergar's.

Though Hughes only bowled first-change on the 1989 tour, he was very much the spearhead when it came to sledging. A young Mike Atherton found that 'I couldn't make out what he was saying, except that every sledge ended with "arsewipe".' Hughes's main target was Robin Smith, the only England batsman with the bottle to hold out for long. 'Mate,' he would say, 'if you just turn the bat over you'll find the instructions on the back.' Or: 'Does your husband play cricket as well?' One less imaginative offering, 'You can't f***ing bat', came back with interest when Smith unleashed one of his favourite square-cuts for four. 'Hey Merv,' he yelled. 'We make a fine pair, don't we? I can't f***ing bat and you can't f***ing bowl.'

Once the fast men had softened England up, Border used the smiling assassin, Terry Alderman, to administer the *coup de grâce*.

> ## 'Mate, if you just turn the bat over you'll find the instructions on the back.'
> ### Merv Hughes sledges England's Robin Smith

'In my day 58 beers between London and Sydney would have virtually classified you as a teetotaller.'

Ian Chappell, misinformed about Boon's 52-tin feat, plays the curmudgeon

David Boon leads the singing of the team song: 'Under the Southern Cross I stand / A sprig of wattle in my hand / A native in my native land / Australia, you f***ing beauty'

'THATCHER OUT!'
'lbw Alderman 0'
Toilet graffiti, 1989

There was something uncanny about the fixed grin on Alderman's face as he released the ball. Many an opponent walked to the crease wondering what he had to be so pleased about. The answer was soon evident when the ball thudded into their pads and the finger of doom was instantly raised. Judging by his 19 lbws during the 1989 series, Alderman had the umpires under a form of Jedi mind control.

Alderman's wicket-to-wicket method was too much for England's experienced opener Graham Gooch, who stepped down from the team for the fifth Test to get his game straight. Bumping into a group of journalists, he remarked sarcastically: 'I'm just off to the nets to practise my falling-over shot.' But the manoeuvre didn't help: Gooch was lbw Alderman 0 at The Oval as well.

Australia set a number of records that summer, none more celebrated than David Boon's feat of drinking 52 tinnies on the flight from Sydney to London. The 'keg on legs' got the tour off to a rip-roaring start when he broke the 44-tin mark set by his lookalike, Rod Marsh. He then spent the best part of two days asleep, missed two training sessions, and copped a hefty fine from the team management. The government of Tasmania – Boon's home state – was once reported to have considered lowering the speed limit to 52kph in tribute.

REVENGE OF THE AMATEURS

England's shortcomings reached all the way up to the old–school-tie brigade at Lord's. While post–Packer Australia had finally put its house in order, the people running – or should that be ruining? – the English game were still a bunch of doddering amateurs.

The committee-men dropped a major clanger at the start of the summer, when they refused to countenance Mike Gatting's return as captain. In their rheumy eyes, Gatting was a working-class oik who had besmirched the name of English cricket. First he had shouted at a Pakistani umpire, and then he had invited a barmaid up to his room during the Nottingham Test of 1988. This was no way for an English gentleman to behave.

Gatting's appointment was formally vetoed by Ossie Wheatley, chairman of the English board. It was a terrible waste of talent. Admittedly, Gatting's Test record was patchy, but he was the kind of pugnacious character you could imagine leading the troops over the barbed wire. At the very least he would have put some spine into the team. Instead, the job went to Gower – a man with a private education, a deliciously fluid batting style, and all the motivational flair of a lemon meringue.

Whenever things got sticky – as they often did in 1989 – Gower defaulted into ironic mode. This technique would come in handy after his retirement, notably during Gower's eight-season stint on BBC TV's satirical sports quiz *They Think It's All Over*. As an England captain, however, his schoolboy humour tended to fall flat. There was a typical instance in 1986, when Peter May

> **'They bring him out of the loft, take the dust sheet off him, give him a pink gin and sit him there. He can't go out of a 30-mile radius of London because he's normally too pissed to get back.'**
>
> Ian Botham on the average England selector, 1986

accused Gower of floating around ineffectually. Gower's response was to have 13 T-shirts printed, one saying 'I'm In Charge', and the other 12 'I'm Not'. He was sacked at the end of the match, creating an excellent photo opportunity when he handed the 'I'm In Charge' T-shirt to Gatting on the England balcony. (The two big G's performed a *pas de deux* throughout the mid-1980s: if one of them wasn't captain, the other usually was.)

Gower's most memorable contributions to the 1989 series came at press conferences. At Edgbaston, a series of simple questions reduced him to banging his forehead on the table, Basil Fawlty-style. At Lord's, his former team-mate Phil Edmonds riled him even more severely by suggesting that he had bowled everyone from the wrong end. Gower simply stood up, announced that he had a taxi waiting, and stalked off to watch the Cole Porter musical *Anything Goes*. If this was Gower's idea of a V-sign, at least it was the kind of V-sign of which Ossie Wheatley might have approved.

Perhaps 1989 was just a star-crossed summer for England. Everything they tried backfired. To take one example, Phil Newport was handed his debut in the first Test, after bowling Worcestershire to victory over the Aussies in a warm-up match. He had done the damage by swinging the big-seamed Reader ball around corners. But Gower – in one of his more laid-back moments – went along with Border's preference for the more batsman-friendly Duke ball. Sure enough, when Newport came on to bowl, the Duke behaved just like the one in the song – up and down, up and down. He took two for plenty as Australia declared on 601 for seven.

Whose team is it anyway? David Gower and Mike Gatting took turns to captain England during the 1980s, with limited success

The series was a fiery baptism for England's new chairman of selectors, Ted Dexter. If May had left him an ageing team in 1961, a dearth of decent fast bowlers in the late 1980s made for an even bleaker legacy. The season started with a rash of injuries, notably Botham's fractured cheekbone after a missed hook against Glamorgan, and ended with a full squad of players signing for Mike Gatting's rebel tour to South Africa. The names were announced on the last day of the fifth Test. In the England dressing-room, Angus Fraser said to Atherton: 'This is unbelievable. Surely playing for your country is meant to mean more than this.'

'Gower is the most disastrous leader since Ethelred the Unready. Beyond question he should now stand down in favour of Ken Dodd.'

The Sun, summer 1989

One could hardly blame Gatting for defecting, after the way he had been treated, but the scramble to find 11 fit and available bodies for The Oval almost brought English cricket to its knees. At one point the team manager, Micky Stewart, told reporters that the latest call-up, Kent's Alan Igglesden, was England's 17th-choice seamer – a vote of confidence if ever there was one. The total number of players used that summer reached 29, one short of the 1921 record.

Dexter was a great one for thinking outside the box, sometimes even outside the planet. When the team gathered before the third Test, he handed out sheets featuring a morale-boosting team song – self-penned, of course – and told the players:

1989: 6 TESTS
AUSTRALIA 4–0

M.A. TAYLOR (AUS.) 838 runs at 83.90

T.M. ALDERMAN (AUS.) 41 wkts at 17.36

Steve Waugh set the tone, scoring 393 runs in five innings before he was dismissed. Then Mark Taylor took over, piling up the biggest aggregate since Bradman, and sharing an opening stand of 329 with Geoff Marsh at Trent Bridge. The Ashes were surrendered tamely, the batting of newcomer Robin Smith (554 runs at 61.44) providing England's sole consolation.

'Who can forget Malcolm Devon?'

England's chairman of selectors Ted Dexter
salutes Devon Malcolm

'Right lads, when you get in the bath tonight, I want you to sing this at the top of your voices.'

'Onward Gower's cricketers,' the first verse started, 'Striving for a score / With our bats uplifted / We want more and more / Alderman the master / Represents the foe / Forward into battle / Down the pitch we go.'

Dexter was not just madcap, he was absurdly gaffe-prone, spending more time with his foot in his mouth than the average tabby cat. The best of the bunch came at Trent Bridge, when he was asked whether there had been any positives to come out of the match. His response – 'Who can forget Malcolm Devon?' – would have been a brilliant wisecrack if only he had said it on purpose.

'I've faced bigger, uglier bowlers than you mate, now f*** off and bowl the next one.'

Allan Border to England's Angus Fraser, who had sledged
him for playing and missing

DAVID GOWER'S FLYING CIRCUS

The 1990–91 Ashes threw up another clash of cultures, this time within the England camp. There was Gooch, the eternal roundhead, desperately trying to pull his team up by its bootstraps. And there was Gower, the blond cavalier, spending late nights at casinos and buzzing the ground in a Tiger Moth. It was a wonder that Australia did not win by a bigger margin than 3–0.

The Tiger Moth incident summed up the tour. England were already two down in the Tests with two to play, but a game against Queensland was going swimmingly, and the mood in the dressing-room was unusually buoyant. When Gower mentioned that he fancied taking to the air, he was joined by one of the young bucks in the squad, John Morris. They hopped across the road to the adjacent Carrara airport. A few minutes later, they were saluting Robin Smith's hundred from the air.

'A fart competing with thunder.'

England captain Graham Gooch on the 1990–91 Ashes series

The trouble started when the press cottoned on. Next morning, Gooch and the tour manager, Peter Lush, summoned Gower to an impromptu court-martial. 'You can either be heavy about it, or you can treat it as a harmless prank,' said Gower, knowing full well which way they were about to go. Gooch replied, in that doleful way of his: 'I don't think you enjoy this game very much, Lubo.' Gower enjoyed it even less after a £1,000 fine and a brusque statement from Lush: 'Immature, ill-

David Gower and John Morris pose for ill-advised press photos in a Tiger Moth. A £1,000 fine and a dressing-down awaited These Magnificent Miscreants in Their Flying Machines

judged and ill-timed.' He would probably have been sent home but for the fact that he was one of England's few batsmen in form.

In the next Test, Gower walked out to the middle to the tune of 'Those Magnificent Men In Their Flying Machines'. He then made a scratchy 11 before being dismissed off the last ball before lunch, flipping a lazy leg-side pick-up to a man placed behind square for exactly that purpose. As Atherton wrote: 'I think it was the last straw for [Gooch] and Gower played only intermittently after that.'

This was the also the tour when the Australians discovered the constant source of merriment that was Philip Clive Roderick

D.C. BOON (AUS.) 520 runs at 75.71

B.A. REID (AUS.) 27 wkts at 16.00

England now had Micky Stewart as a sergeant-majorish coach but what they really needed was a team doctor: Gooch missed the first Test with a poisoned finger, Lamb tore a calf jogging back to the hotel, and Fraser suffered the first twinges of a career-threatening hip injury. Australia offered twin spearheads in Craig McDermott, a Queensland budgie-breeder, and Bruce Reid, a left-armer built like a pipe-cleaner.

Tufnell. When bowling his left-arm spin, Tufnell had an elegant, smooth, Rolls Royce of an action. When fielding in the deep, he was more like a Thunderbird puppet missing a couple of strings. One banner in the crowd saluted 'The Phil Tufnell Fielding Academy'.

When a wit's-end Gooch turned to Ian Chappell for advice, he was told: 'Bowl him more often. At least that way he won't be fielding.' Yet even this was no safeguard against a Tufnell brainstorm. In a one-day game at Sydney, the man they call the artful dropper managed to fluff a guaranteed run-out by fumbling a gentle underarm return, then picking the ball up and throwing it violently past the stumps. Steve Waugh, who had been peeling off his gloves, was able to jog back into his ground.

No England tourist since Douglas Jardine has attracted more heckles from the bleachers. Tufnell heard all the classics. 'Hey,

'Tufnell! Can I borrow your brain? I'm building an idiot.'

Australian barracker to Phil Tufnell

Phil Tufnell enjoys a gargle and a gasper. In the words of Barry
Norman, he was 'the archetypal fag-puffing, beer-swilling, bird-pulling,
bouncer-evading village cricketer who lurked, rather than fielded, in
the deep yet somehow made it into the big time'

'You've got to bat on this in a minute, Tufnell. Hospital food suit you?'

Australian fast bowler Craig McDermott after being dismissed by Phil Tufnell, 1991

Tufnell, where do you keep your savings – under the soap?' Or: 'The best thing about you, Tufnell, is still dribbling down your mother's legs.' These were time-honoured refrains, lavished on every England new boy over the last few decades. But at least he was honoured by the invention of one fresh line: 'Tufnell! Can I borrow your brain? I'm building an idiot.'

Tufnell must have known he was struggling when the umpires started to sledge him. In his autobiography, he relates the story of how he turned to Peter McConnell at Melbourne to ask how many balls were left in the over. 'Count them yourself, you Pommy c***,' McConnell replied. Even Tufnell, who liked to paint himself as a cheeky cockney chappie from norf London, was rendered momentarily speechless.

As Tufnell's jaw dropped, Gooch walked over to offer a rare display of support. 'I heard what you said,' he told McConnell, 'and you cannot talk to my players like that.' The sting in the tail came when David Boon nicked a thick edge through to wicketkeeper Jack Russell. Tufnell describes turning in triumph to McConnell, who 'looked me straight in the eye and said: "Not out." "You f***ing bastard," I said. "Now you can't talk to me like that, Phil," he replied.'

THE BALL OF THE CENTURY

There were more than 15,000 balls bowled during the 1993 series, but most people remember only one. When Shane Warne dismissed Mike Gatting with his first delivery in Ashes cricket, he created an iconic sporting moment. He also placed England in a psychological half-nelson that lingers to this day.

Warne came into the series as little more than a chubby wannabe. A failed Aussie Rules footballer, and former pizza delivery boy, his early experiments with leg-spin had not inspired much confidence. 'You haven't got it, son,' was the considered verdict of Mike Tamblyn, his captain at Brighton CC in Melbourne.

Even when he sneaked into the Australian Academy, Warne's attempts to master the dreaded flipper – the hardest delivery in cricket – were less than promising. 'He used to hit the side of the net, the roof, everything,' said his coach, Jack Potter. 'At one stage he said to me, "I'll never be able to bowl this."'

Then came Gatting. This was an orthodox leg-break, which hummed dangerously as it flicked out of Warne's fleshy fingers. It started out on a middle-stump line, before drifting in towards Gatting's pads, hitting the ground, changing direction, skewing back past his front leg and clipping the top of his off stump. Here was cricket's equivalent of the laser-guided missile that turns left once inside the front door. Because the victim was Gatting, a man built even more comfortably than Warne himself, the dismissal sparked off a feast of one-liners.

> **'You haven't got it, son.'**
> Melbourne club side captain
> to the young Shane Warne

'If it had been a cheese roll, it would never have got past him,' quipped Gooch. 'The last time I saw that look on Gatt's face, someone had nicked his lunch,' chimed Tufnell. The cricket writer Martin Johnson trumped them both with: 'How anyone can spin a ball the width of Gatting boggles the mind.'

The 'Ball of the Century' was certainly the making of Warne, a man whose blond highlights had earned him the nickname 'Hollywood'. Warne has always been a showy sort of character; as the Australian idiom has it, he is as flash as a rat with a gold tooth. And now he had something to be flash about. 'In the space of one delivery so much had changed,' he recalled. 'My confidence was sky-high. I was pumped up and rock 'n' rolling.'

It may just be another Pommie excuse, but the writer and theorist Scyld Berry has often argued that the Gooch–Gower feud proved costly at this moment. If England had picked their best team, they would have had Gower at No. 3 and the ball would have spun harmlessly into his front pad. Instead, Warne's dramatic way of introducing himself seemed to scramble English brains.

The best parallel here is with 1981. Just as Botham's Headingley miracle had convinced Australians that he could do anything, anywhere, any time, so Warne's wonder-ball gave him an aura that he never lost. Even when he bowled a long-hop, there was a temptation to think it was all part of some masterplan. Not that he often did, of course. While Botham was erratic by nature, Warne turned out to be that rarest of beasts, an attacking wrist-spinner who hardly bowled a loose ball.

If there is one single reason why England had to wait another 12 years to win the Ashes back, it wore gold ear-rings and liked a cheeseburger. Warne had the lot, including natural blond roots. His technique was immaculate, his nerve was unflappable, and his reading of the game should have made him Australian captain. The only problem was his long series of off-field indiscretions. From the administrators' perspective, Warne was the modern equivalent of Keith Miller,

'If it had been a cheese roll, it would never have got past him.'

Graham Gooch on Mike Gatting's dismissal by Warne's 'ball of the century'

You've been Warned: Shane Warne bowls a disbelieving
Mike Gatting, who insisted on checking with the umpire
before he would leave the pitch

'Shane Warne's idea of a balanced diet is a cheeseburger in each hand.'

Australian wicketkeeper

Ian Healy, 1996

an unpredictable scamp with a taste for trouble.

Warne's catalogue of scrapes began with the cash-for-answers scandal (when he and Mark Waugh received A$5,000 for pitch and weather information in Pakistan in 1994) and continued with his positive drugs test before the 2003 World Cup (which he blamed on a slimming pill given to him by his mum). He also suffers – if that is the right word – from a hyperactive libido. According to the author of a recent unauthorised biography, 'One of Warne's mates at Channel 9 told me he reckoned Warne had a pretty good average because he had probably had 1000 women and only been caught five times.'

Warne's colourful lifestyle was described by another acquaintance as 'morally dyslexic'. It caught up with him in 1999, when he was accused of sending sleazy text messages to a Leicester nurse. At that point, the Australian board grew tired of Warne putting the vice into vice-captain. They passed the job on to Adam Gilchrist instead, a paragon of integrity who defied every preconception about Aussie cricketers when he started walking for thin edges.

In his autobiography, a frustrated Warne turned to 1970s TV for a coded take on the affair: 'We do not want a Richie Cunningham figure in charge unless he is the best person,' Warne wrote. 'He was the character in *Happy Days*, who was always polite and well-mannered, who said the right thing at the right time, but relied on the Fonz, a more confident, streetwise figure, to overcome his problems in the real world.' Gilchrist is understood to have been less than impressed by the implication.

A WORD
IN YOUR EAR

Warne was an instant phenomenon, but even he could not have scattered England so thoroughly without Merv Hughes bumping and bustling away at the other end. Looking increasingly like the villain in a silent movie, Hughes put such a massive effort into the 1993 series that it virtually finished his career.

Already plagued by gammy knees, Hughes ended up bowling 296 overs for 31 wickets in the six Tests. He relied on anti-inflammatories, ice treatment and gallows humour to overcome the pain. According to Warne: 'He said that if he ever needed five ice-packs instead of the usual four it was time to retire.'

This was the kind of commitment that Border could wring from his players, and it contrasted dramatically with the listless feel of England's ragtag army. 'Our unwritten motto was "Play hard, party hard",' wrote Steve Waugh, 'while the Poms' seemed to be "Compete, then disappear".'

England's great white hope was the naturalised Zimbabwean, Graeme Hick, who had scored a maiden Test hundred in Bombay the previous winter. Built like a rugby flank-forward, Hick was an imposing sight at the crease, yet he never imposed himself on international cricket. His story was one of seven years' feast with Worcestershire, while he waited to qualify for England, followed by a decade of relative famine as a Test batsman.

Neither the peace of his parents' tobacco farm nor the dreaming spire of Worcester Cathedral could have prepared Hick for the rough-house treatment he got from international bowlers.

Merv Hughes torments the hapless Graeme Hick. 'He would sledge his own mother if he thought it would help the cause,' said former England fast bowler Gladstone Small

Robin Smith was sympathetic, arguing that everyone 'wanted to get out the next Don Bradman. When I was batting with him and standing at the non-striker's end I thought I was playing in a different game.' But the selectors – and, crucially, the captain – pointed towards a failure of temperament. 'The only time I can remember Hick sledging on the field was when he came on as substitute,' Atherton wrote, 'because there was no chance of him being sledged back at the crease.'

Whichever side you come down on in the great Hick debate, there is no doubt that the 1993 Ashes produced one of the most sustained campaigns of verbal intimidation ever seen. Every time

Hick came out to bat, there was Hughes's absurd moustache, tickling his ear. It didn't even stop when he was out: one classic photograph shows Hughes still screaming at him as he walks off.

Like Lillee before him, Hughes claimed this was all in a day's work. 'In 1993 [Hick] was a real danger, we made no bones about it, and the fast bowlers did target him,' he said. 'Because Graeme had such fantastic ability, we would test him in other ways. If you are struggling mentally then you will be put under scrutiny.' The extra attention clearly worked. Hick was out to Hughes

1993: 6 TESTS
AUSTRALIA 4–1

S.K. WARNE (AUS.) — 34 wkts at 25.79

G.A. GOOCH (ENG.) — 673 runs at 56.08

An ever-mutating England seam attack made scant impression on hungry Australian batsmen, of whom six scored more than 400 runs. For England, the 40-year-old Gooch's Indian summer continued unabated. Victory at The Oval under Atherton gave England the solace of a first Ashes Test win since 1987.

'Hey, hey, hey, hey! I'm f***ing talking to you. Do that again and you're on the next plane home, son. What was that? You f***ing test me and you'll see.'
Allan Border lays down the law to Craig McDermott, Australia's sulking strike bowler, Taunton, 1993

> **'I am not talking to anyone in the British media – they are all pricks.'**
>
> Allan Border, 1993

three times in a row, and promptly dropped after the second Test. While you had to admire Australia's utter commitment, there was a feeling they had pushed the envelope to its limits. The 1994 *Wisden* criticised Border for 'condoning, and not infrequently participating in, the sledging of opponents and umpires'.

Having given Hick the flick, England's selectors turned to more imported talent. Their new-ball attack at Trent Bridge consisted of Andrew Caddick (born in Christchurch, New Zealand) and Martin McCague (raised in Port Hedland, Western Australia). 'It takes the gloss off an Ashes Test,' griped Border. Most of his compatriots simply found England's desperation laughable. One reporter dubbed McCague 'the rat who joined the sinking ship'.

Experimentation was necessary, as a golden generation was on the wane. Botham and Gower both retired in 1993, in a huff at their non-selection. Dexter was off, too, though not before one last PR disaster after the Lord's Test. Asked if he could explain England's seventh successive defeat, he replied: 'Maybe we are in the wrong sign. Maybe Venus is in the wrong juxtaposition with something else. I don't know.'

Dexter's last act was to appoint Atherton as captain, with a mandate for change. While this was a popular move, it could not make up for four years of malapropisms and rum hunches. During the final Test, Jonathan Agnew told listeners to *Test Match Special*: 'For those of you wondering what that round of applause was, it was to mark the resignation of Ted Dexter.'

CAPTAIN GRUMPY

Mike Atherton was England's longest-serving captain, and also one of the most oppressed men in sport. As David Lloyd George once said of Lord Derby, his minister for war, 'Like a cushion, he always bore the impress of the last man who sat on him.'

It was Atherton's fate to play throughout the longest spell of Australian domination in Ashes history. Of eight series in their winning run, he appeared in seven and captained in four. He kept coming back, even after his spine had locked up and made it impossible for him to duck Glenn McGrath's bouncers. Steve Waugh compared him to a cockroach, because he simply refused to crawl away and die.

There was a bit of edge between these two. After the 1993 series, Atherton said: 'The one who really got up my nose was Steve Waugh, who spent the entire series giving out verbals – a bit of a joke really when he was the one bloke wetting himself against the quick bowlers.'

This was a rare instance of a big statement from Atherton, who soon regretted it when the 1994–95 Ashes came around. He has described walking out for his first innings, whereupon Waugh immediately volunteered to field at silly point. '"I've waited a long time for this," he snarled, as he took up residence under my nose, and he continued to growl and snarl throughout my stay.'

Atherton's record looks modest now (7,728 Test runs at just 37.31), but there are many reasons why he deserves a generous epitaph. As a batsman, he opened the innings in a period of lethal fast-bowling duos. As a captain, he was constantly battling against the retro instincts of Raymond Illingworth, the chairman of selectors.

'If the Poms win the toss and bat, keep the taxi running.'
Australian crowd banner, 1994–95

1994–95: 5 TESTS
AUSTRALIA 3–1

M.J. SLATER (AUS.) | 623 runs at 62.30

C.J. McDERMOTT (AUS.) | 32 wkts at 21.09

Phil DeFreitas's first ball – which Michael Slater panned to the cover fence – set the tone for two early walkovers, but England rallied through Darren Gough's six-for at Sydney. They might even have won that game if Atherton had not flattened team morale by declaring with Hick on 98. At Adelaide, the tourists did win, with a team fashioned from the last 11 fit players in the squad. But the final Test found them crumbling to 123 all out in pursuit of 453, demolished by McDermott and new fast-bowling discovery Glenn McGrath. Warne claimed a hat-trick at Melbourne – the first in Ashes Tests for 90 years.

And on top of all that, he was physically handicapped by a genetic back condition called ankylosing spondylitis. No wonder they called him Captain Grumpy.

Atherton's first Ashes series as captain, in 1994–95, was a shocker from the moment the team was picked. Illingworth insisted on taking both Gooch (41) and Gatting (37). Dennis Lillee also made a comeback, but only for the traditional tour opener at Lilac Hill, when he stopped in mid-run and yelled: 'Hell, Gatt, move out of the way. I can't see the stumps.' During a state match a few days later, Atherton was alarmed by the sight of the two dinosaurs grazing at mid-on and mid-off: 'I knew then that it was going to be a long, long tour.'

It was also a tour of bizarre ailments. Devon Malcolm contracted chickenpox, Joey Benjamin was wrongly diagnosed with shingles,

'It must stand for Overwhelmingly Beaten Englishman.'

Ian Chadband, when Gooch was awarded an OBE after England had lost the 1994–95 Ashes series

and Tufnell had a breakdown. Not the kind of physical breakdown usually associated with English bowlers on tour, but a full-blown freak-out. When his second wife told him she was having second thoughts about their marriage, Tufnell entered a trough of depression, trashed his hotel room and had to be checked into a psychiatric institution.

After leaving Tufnell in care, Atherton and tour manager M.J.K. Smith had just returned to the hotel and were deciding on a replacement when there was a knock on the door. 'To my eternal astonishment,' Atherton wrote, 'there stood Tufnell, beer in hand, fag in mouth. He walked in aggressively and proceeded to do a kind of Michael Barrymore impression: "Awright? You awright? I'm awright!" He had discharged himself from hospital and put us in an invidious position.'

Atherton did eventually notch a couple of wins at either end of the 1997 Ashes. The series concluded with a masterclass from the ever-unpredictable Tufnell, who took 11 wickets and then sat silently through the dressing-room celebrations with a towel over his head. Yet England's 3–2 defeat was still a disappointment after a pulsating victory in the opening Test of Edgbaston – the only 'live' Test, in the sense of the Ashes still being at stake, that Australia lost between 1989 and 2005.

The tourists were struggling a little at that stage, and none more so than their captain, Mark Taylor. At the immigration desk at Heathrow, Taylor had received the kind of welcome more often bestowed on Englishmen on their arrival Down Under. 'Mark Taylor, eh? The Australian captain,' said the official. 'But for how long?' Taylor was indeed considering resigning halfway through the first Test at Edgbaston. Australia had been bowled

> '. . . a makeshift outfit that couldn't win an argument with a drover's dog.'
>
> Jeff Thomson on England's bowling attack, 1997

M.T.G. ELLIOTT (AUS.) 556 runs at 55.60

G.D. McGRATH (AUS.) 36 wkts at 19.47

England scored an early upset, but Steve Waugh's twin tons at Old Trafford resumed normal service. Graham Thorpe then dropped a pivotal slip catch off Elliott at Headingley, and Warne celebrated the retention of the Ashes at Trent Bridge with a hip-wiggling victory dance. England had been crushed yet again by vastly superior opponents, whose skill and remorselessness was embodied by the outstanding McGrath.

> **'When the pressure point comes, English cricketers crumble.'**
>
> Shane Warne, 1997

out for 118, of which he had made seven. The *Daily Mirror* had also been following him around with a bat a metre wide, prompting him to remark: 'I don't think I need to pose with an oversized bat to prove I have a sense of humour.' But Taylor, backed by wife Judy to score a hundred at odds of 25–1, did exactly that in the second innings. Australia still lost by nine wickets, but as Taylor put it: 'We had got rid of our one big problem – me.'

It was comfortable enough in the end, as Australia continued their sequence of introducing one unarguably great player to England every time they visited. There was Steve Waugh in 1989, Shane Warne in 1993 – and there would be Adam Gilchrist in 2001. But the 1997 model was Glenn McGrath, as tall, angry and implacable as a desert dust-storm. Atherton certainly reaped the whirlwind, falling to McGrath seven times in 12 innings.

This was a series of tight margins – tighter, at least, than was normal in the 1990s. England were all convinced that Steve Waugh was plumb lbw at Old Trafford on 0, but had to stifle their curses as Waugh went on to 108. In a similar situation at Headingley, Thorpe dropped a sitter off Matthew Elliott at slip. Once Elliott had completed a savage innings of 199, a glum Atherton paraphrased Gubby Allen's great line from 1936–37 (see page 122): 'Don't worry, Thorpey, you've only cost us the Ashes.'

Fat Boy Spin's Ashes victory dance, 1997. Warne would still be pestering England's cricketers (and occasionally England's women) eight years later

1998–99: 5 TESTS
AUSTRALIA 3–1

S.R. WAUGH (AUS.)	498 runs at 83.00
S.C.G. MACGILL (AUS.)	27 wkts at 17.70

After a drawn first Test, victories at Perth and Adelaide saw Australia retain the Ashes before Christmas — something never done before. But England could have gone away with a drawn series if Peter Such's bum hadn't obscured the side-on cameras at a crucial moment in Sydney. Michael Slater survived the run-out appeal to score 123, and Gough's marvellous hat-trick went unrewarded.

WAUGH'S AUSSIES: INVINCIBLE OR UNSPEAKABLE?

When sledged by an opposition quick, Allan Border's favourite response was: 'I've faced bigger, uglier bowlers than you mate, now f★★★ off and bowl the next one.' It was Border's spiritual successor, Steve Waugh, who built one of the biggest, ugliest Australian teams of them all.

Despite Warne's captaincy ambitions, Waugh was the obvious choice to succeed Taylor. For much of the 1990s, he had been the driving force in Australia's side; what rugby players call the pack leader. In 2001, he finally got his chance to lead Australia on an Ashes tour, and did so with narrow-eyed fanaticism, setting an almost superhuman example when he returned from a calf strain to score a century on one leg at The Oval.

Totally committed to making the most of his own ability, Waugh was a self-help book in human form. After a scratchy start in Test cricket, he kept evolving his technique and sharpening his mental disciplines, until he could almost will himself to greatness. His powers of concentration would have put a Buddhist monk to shame.

In a rare moment of détente on the 1998–99 tour, Nasser Hussain asked Waugh about his methods. 'Waugh said, "A lot

'A six-foot blond-haired beach bum bowling at 90mph trying to knock your head off and then telling you you're a feeble-minded tosser – where's the problem?'

Michael Atherton before the 2001 Ashes series

of my batting is about bravado. I go out there and let the bowler and everyone else know that I'm there, rushing to the wicket and sticking my chest out."' Hussain added: 'I felt like saying: "There's a bit more to it than that, Steve," but I knew what he meant.'

Looking down from his Olympian peak of achievement, Steve Waugh loved to pour scorn on English failings and fecklessness. He was particularly gleeful when Nasser Hussain broke a finger in the first Test of 2001, and alternative captaincy candidates such as Alec Stewart and Mark Butcher immediately ruled themselves out. 'I don't think you'd find anyone in the Australian side saying: "I don't want to captain,"' he crowed.

Hussain himself grew increasingly sick of Steve Waugh's homilies. 'He became a bit of a preacher,' Hussain wrote. 'A bit righteous. It was like he expected everyone to do it the Aussie way because their way was the only way. Well, yes, it's the only way if you have Glenn McGrath, Shane Warne, Jason Gillespie, Adam Gilchrist and the rest of them in your team, but we lesser mortals have to do things a different way.'

The 2001 Aussies were certainly a fine vintage. They earned comparisons with Bradman's Invincibles, and would probably have inflicted a whitewash but for the rain that forced a risky declaration at Headingley. Yet many observers felt that their behaviour failed to live up to the standard of their cricket. Neil Harvey, the youngest member of the original 1948 Invincibles, was Waugh's most vocal critic. At the height of Australia's success,

> **'As far as I'm concerned, they are the greatest bunch of sledgers there's ever been.'**
> Former Aussie batting great Neil Harvey on the 2001 Australians

2001: 5 TESTS
AUSTRALIA 4–1

G.D. McGRATH (AUS.)   32 wkts at 16.93

S.K. WARNE (AUS.)   31 wkts at 18.70

Australia just went on getting better and better . . . and better. Overwhelming victories in the first three Tests secured them the Ashes in just 11 days of cricket. England won at Headingley, thanks to Mark Butcher's brilliant 173 not out, only to be crushed by an innings at The Oval. The excellence of McGrath and Warne and the consistency of Australia's top order was now scarily complemented by the presence at No. 7 of rampaging wicketkeeper-batsman Adam Gilchrist (340 runs at 68.00 in the series including a bloodcurdling 152 off 143 balls at Edgbaston).

he told a reporter: 'As far as I'm concerned, they are the greatest bunch of sledgers there's ever been. These boys get into a bit of trouble and it all comes out, every bit of badness in them. All I can say is I'm disgusted and the sad thing is I'm not the only one.'

With his Clint Eastwood eyes and poker face, Waugh was a great exponent of the sledger's art (which he referred to euphemistically as 'mental disintegration'). Waugh's Australians felt it was all part of the game, and had little respect for men, like Hick, who backed away from the challenge. As Waugh himself admitted: 'The opposition players who did well against Australia during my career were the ones with a combative spirit, who weren't submissive but rather enjoyed the gamesmanship and unrelenting pressure.'

Like Ian Chappell, Steve Waugh did not often get involved in a direct confrontation, but as his regular target Mike Atherton put it, 'He would often pass comment to a team-mate, designed of course for the opposition player and within his earshot. "Hey, Warnie," he might say, as he passed Nasser mid-pitch, "Hussain plays with a really open face, doesn't he?"'

There was a range of instruments in this orchestra. At the start of his captaincy career, Waugh had Ian Healy behind the stumps, chuntering away in his gravelly Queensland drawl. 'Back to the nets, dickhead,' was a favourite of Healy's, particularly for batsmen conned by a Warne special. He also memorably told a fielder to stand 'right under Nasser's nose', and then placed him yards away at short extra cover.

Steve Waugh in his battered Baggy Green Cap. Having tasted the bitterness of Ashes defeat in 1986–87, the elder Waugh twin became a lifelong abstainer. 'With the possible exception of Rolf Harris, no other Australian has inflicted more pain and grief on Englishmen since Don Bradman,' said Mike Walters in the *Daily Mirror*

'F*** me, look who it is. Mate, what are you doing out here? There's no way you're good enough to play for England.'
'Maybe not, but at least I'm the best player in my family.'

Exchange between Mark Waugh and England debutant
James Ormond, The Oval, 2001

Then there was McGrath, a man whose bush-town upbringing gave him plenty of what the locals call 'mongrel'. Before each series, McGrath would give an interview announcing which English batsman he was going to lord it over. If he encountered even an iota of resistance, he would start scowling

2002–03: 5 TESTS
AUSTRALIA 4–1

M.L. HAYDEN (AUS.) — 496 runs at 62.00

M.P. VAUGHAN (ENG.) — 633 runs at 63.30

Nasser Hussain chose to field at Brisbane on the first day of the series and watched Hayden and Ponting rack up 362 for two. From then on, it was all downhill for England. Massive victories there, at Adelaide and at Perth gave the Ashes to Australia by the first day of December, then England scored their customary consolation win at Sydney. The elegant Michael Vaughan scored three big centuries in the series, while Steve Waugh brought his Ashes career to an appropriate close with a fairytale 102 in the final Test, completed off the last ball of the second day.

and snarling away like a road-rage head-case. In the words of the England coach David Lloyd, McGrath possessed 'a common trait of Australian cricketers by being a lovely chap off the field but thoroughly nasty when he has the ball in his hands. He boils over, becomes abusive, loses the plot.'

'Back to the nets, dickhead.'
Australian wicketkeeper Ian Healy's favourite sledge to a just-dismissed batsman

While McGrath cussed the batsman from one end, Warne enticed him from the other. Atherton has described how in the third Test of 2001, Warne taunted the obdurate Mark Ramprakash, saying: 'Come on Ramps, you know you want to!' and 'That's the way Ramps, keep coming down the wicket.' Eventually Ramprakash took the bait, launched a humungous heave, and was stumped. He had been hooked, reeled in, and cooked with lemon on the barbie.

'Is there anyone in England who can play cricket?'
Headline in Sydney's *Daily Telegraph*, 2002–2003

McGrath and Warne were Australia's champions through the Waugh era – a post-watershed version of Davidson and Benaud. Yet this strength could also be a weakness. The 2005 series would show what could happen when one of the Big Two went missing . . .

THE URN RETURNS

There was a sense of history in the air on the morning of 4 August 2005. Only minutes before the second Test was due to start, Glenn McGrath turned his ankle on a loose ball. (Loose balls and McGrath never did go well together.) Then Ricky Ponting confounded all expectations by asking England to bat first. His decision will be remembered as one of the most infamous insertions since Brutus did for Caesar.

Here was opportunity in abundance. But would England be good enough, or brave enough, to take it? Over the previous 16 years, they had seemed almost allergic to Ashes success.

But the difference this time lay in the personnel. Michael Vaughan was leading a fresh young England side, free of the scars that had afflicted the previous generation. Vaughan himself had marmalised Australia's bowlers in 2002–03, so he had no wounds to hide. Together with Duncan Fletcher, England's latest coach, he hatched a plan to take the fight to the opposition – to 'get in their space', as Fletcher put it.

England laid down a marker in the very first match – a Twenty20 game of all things. After striking Andrew Symonds on the shoulder with a bouncer, Darren Gough fixed him with a red-faced, barrel-chested glare worthy of John Bull himself. It was a telling start to the summer. Then, on the first morning of the Test series, Steve Harmison inflicted further body blows on Australia's top three. The worst affected was the captain, Ricky Ponting, who needed running repairs after his helmet grille cut a gash in his cheek.

> **'Who do you think you are, Steve Waugh?'**
> Michael Vaughan responds to a Ponting earbashing at Lord's

The old England would have gathered round in sympathy, but Vaughan's men maintained an icy silence. As Justin Langer said to Andrew Strauss, 'This really is a war out here, isn't it? You're not even going up and seeing if he's all right.'

For all England's spiky attitude, they still lost the match by 239 runs. The pundits switched automatically into last-

> **'[Ponting has the] pained expression of a man in urgent need of the nearest toilet.'**
>
> The *Guardian*, July 2005

Ricky Ponting ponders the prospect of becoming the first Australian captain to lose the Ashes since Allan Border in 1986–87. 'Ponting resembles George W. Bush and leads like him too,' said Tim de Lisle in *The Times*

> **'He's a lovely guy, that Ricky Ponting. He likes the English so much he changed the series for them with the most stupid decision he'll ever make in his life.'**
>
> Geoff Boycott gloats at Ponting's insertion of England at Edgbaston

rites mode. But then came Edgbaston, McGrath's ankle, Ponting's decision, and one of the most cathartic days in English cricket history. 'I have a vivid memory of sitting with Strauss on the balcony, doing a Sudoku puzzle, while boundaries were flying everywhere,' Trescothick recalled, at the end of the summer. 'We agreed that it was like watching a benefit match. Australia looked shell-shocked when they came off.' The scoreboard read 407 all out, off just 79.2 overs.

When Brett Lee led a recovery on the fourth morning, one wondered whether England would ever get the monkey off their backs. After 16 years, it must have felt more like an elephant. But in the end they inched home by two runs – the narrowest victory margin in Ashes history. This was one of those matches in which Andrew Flintoff could do no wrong. He put a consoling arm around Lee at the finish, and created one of the images of the summer.

Was history beckoning for England? An email appeared in many inboxes, drawing parallels between 1981 (which featured a royal wedding, a dead Pope, and a European triumph for Liverpool FC) and 2005 (ditto). The implication – that a Bothamesque all-rounder would drive England to Ashes glory – became more and more plausible as the series wore on. Flintoff was man of the match in both England's wins, at Edgbaston and Trent Bridge, then put everything he had left into a mammoth bowling performance at The Oval. 'It would be nice if we could find an Andrew Flintoff from somewhere,' was Ponting's post-series verdict. 'I'm sure

> **'I call him the new Daryll. He's the new Cullinan, I reckon.'**
>
> Warne compares Andrew Strauss to South Africa's Daryll Cullinan, one of his most regular victims. Strauss responded with two composed hundreds

we'll be looking as soon as we get back home.'

By the fourth Test, Ponting must already have been dreading the potential humiliation of slinking back into Australia without the Ashes, rather in the manner of a teenager tiptoeing into the family home after a late night. His self-control finally cracked when he was run out by a fleet-footed young substitute named Gary Pratt. He left the field in a fury, aiming a flurry of invective at Fletcher, the inscrutable Zimbabwean, who produced a rare smile in return. Some sources say that he even winked.

The final act belonged to Kevin Pietersen. Another product of southern Africa, Pietersen was a brash young peacock with a

'I'd rather lose to the district women's 2nd team than lose to England.'

A resident of Shane Warne's home suburb of Black Rock watches the final Test of 2005

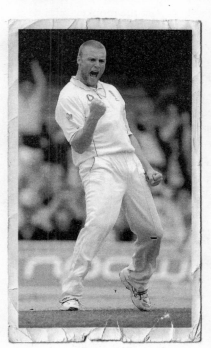

stripy coxcomb to match. He came to the crease with McGrath on a hat-trick and England's whole edifice crumbling away. His response was an innings that few English-born cricketers, labouring under the weight of Ashes history, would even have dreamed of. 'I remember he was faffing around against Warne, then suddenly he went six, six,'

'Freddie' Flintoff celebrates another wicket in a summer when his pace and bounce transfixed the Australians. 'He has a big wrist; he has a big everything,' said Michael Vaughan

> **'Warney, just because you're a mate of Pietersen's, it didn't mean on that last day at The Oval you had to drop him. Do you wake up in the middle of the night thinking you might have dropped the Ashes?'**
>
> Phil Tufnell teases Warne at an awards ceremony
> in Melbourne, February 2006

Flintoff and Pietersen, dubbed the 'TNT twins' by the tabloid press, totter towards 10 Downing Street. Tony Blair and pineapple juice awaited England's Ashes-winning heroes at the end of an epic night's carousing

Trescothick recalled. 'He told me: "I've had enough of blocking – I'm gonna smash it."' Pietersen's mind-boggling 158 from 187 balls contained an Ashes record of seven sixes, one more than Botham hit at Old Trafford in 1981. It was an unorthodox and unforgettable way of saving a vital Test.

At some point during the 24-hour bender that followed – whether on the open-top bus, at the bar of China White's, or during tea at No. 10 – it is tempting to imagine that Vaughan might have turned to Pietersen and said: 'Congratulations, Mr Pietersen, you've just won us the Ashes.'

2005: 5 TESTS
ENGLAND 2–1

A. FLINTOFF (ENG.) — 402 runs at 40.20 & 24 wkts at 27.29

S.K. WARNE (AUS.) — 40 wkts at 19.92

McGrath's progress was crucial to the first three Tests. After nine wickets in a crushing win at Lord's, he felt smug enough to predict a 5–0 whitewash. But his turned ankle at Edgbaston turned the series on its head, with a little help from Flintoff. At Old Trafford, it was his batting that mattered: he and Lee saw out the final four overs to clinch a pulsating draw. Meanwhile, his colleagues had been struggling against England's secret weapon, reverse-swing, purveyed with speed and accuracy by Flintoff and Simon Jones. Australia could perhaps have squared the series if Warne had caught Pietersen on 15 at The Oval. But it was hard to blame a man who took 40 wickets in the series.

THE REVENGERS' TRAGICOMEDY

Only a few hours before England's 2006–07 tourists were due to fly home, their physio Dean Conway was mugged in a hotel lobby by a gang of knife-wielding, balaclava-clad thieves. It was arguably the warmest welcome the England boys had received all trip.

Flintoff and Co. had carried a price on their heads from the moment they raised the replica urn at the Kennington Oval, 18 months earlier. The popular view Down Under was that the Poms had celebrated not wisely, but too well. The ticker tape, the book deals and the New Year's honours had all been perfectly calculated to raise Australian hackles. In 2006–07, the backlash hit England like a tidal wave.

Ponting tried to pretend that it was just another series. When one questioner brought up the subject of revenge, he replied: 'I have never mentioned that word once, not even to myself.' He also claimed that Australia had never consciously targeted a whitewash. But no one really believed him. As far back as September, Brett Lee had been inscribing souvenir cricket balls with the message 'Aust v Eng 2006–07 – 5–0'.

The series shifted close to 800,000 tickets and was widely described as the most hyped Ashes contest in history. Yet this assessment was only half right, as the word 'contest' proved ill-suited to what became a ruthless exercise in subjugation. As Marshal Bosquet said of the Charge of the Light Brigade, '*C'est magnifique, mais ce n'est pas la guerre.*'

Ponting led the way from the very beginning. He opened the series with a flawless 196 – an 'over my dead body' sort of innings.

A muted Pietersen congratulates Shane Warne after Australia's Ashes-winning victory at Perth. The friendship between the Hampshire pair had experienced a blip at the Gabba, when a throw from Warne nearly struck Pietersen on the head, eliciting a response of 'dickhead' from the South African-born batsman

Finally dismissed on the second afternoon, he stormed off in such a temper that he failed to acknowledge a standing ovation. Here was a man with a score to settle, a modern Fury in whites.

Boosted by the arrival of Mike Hussey and Stuart Clark, two late but lavish bloomers, the Aussies matched their captain's zeal. The team's average age of 32.9 might have been the highest of any Australian side since 1928, but what they lacked in hair follicles they made up in discipline, teamwork and know-how.

England, by contrast, had stagnated since their 2005 apotheosis. Their vulnerability was obvious from the very first ball of the series, which squirted out of Steve Harmison's hand as if coated in Vaseline, and flew straight to Flintoff at second slip.

In that one instant, the tour's ignominious trajectory was established. 'Wide They Bother?' screamed the back-page headline in the Sydney *Daily Telegraph*. Harmison admitted afterwards that he had simply frozen in the spotlight. Yet worse was to come in the second Test, where England were gripped by a collective panic that cost them the match, the series, and the respect of the Australian public.

This cataclysm represented England's point of no return. They should never have lost in Adelaide: they had declared their first innings on 551 for six, for goodness sakes, and would have had Australia 78 for four if Ashley Giles (whose controversial selection ahead of Monty Panesar became a *cause célèbre*) had not made an alarmingly geriatric attempt to catch Ponting at deep square-leg.

Instead they allowed Australia to score 513 in return, then spent the final day sleepwalking to 129 all out from 73 overs. It was a collapse in slow-motion, a nightmare of paralysis, as agonising to watch as one of those horror movies where kooky teenagers hole up in a log cabin in the woods.

England's decision-making was equally suspect. They tried to take refuge in strokeless defence, but

'Harmison's first ball . . . could only have been tracked by a satellite device from Cape Canaveral.'
The *Daily Telegraph's* Martin Johnson on Harmy's series-opening wide

Shane Warne played the role of bogeyman, picking off his victims in a variety of outrageous ways.

With English blood staining the water, the feeding frenzy began. At Perth, Adam Gilchrist walloped the fastest Ashes hundred in history. At Melbourne, Andrew Symonds made merry with a maiden Test century of his own. And things were going awry off the field as well. In that same fourth Test, England's bowling plans somehow found their way out of the MCG dressing-room and onto ABC national radio. The commentators had some good sport with the spelling, which was every bit as erratic as the bowling itself.

England's 10-wicket defeat at the SCG completed an unholy quintet. Australia had won 5–0 – the first whitewash in any Ashes series since Warwick Armstrong in 1920–21. Flintoff thus joined J.W.H.T. Douglas in the Hall of Ashes Infamy (and without the excuse of a World War to fall back on). It was a rapid comedown for the hero of 2005: like the unfortunate Dean Conway, he had stumbled into a violent ambush.

> **'Lose toss, bowl England out for not many, score lots more, bowl them out again for not many, go fishing.'**
> The *Observer*'s Kevin Mitchell identifies Australia's winning strategy at the MCG

OH, FOR
FRED'S SAKE

England's 2006–07 tour debacle flowed from the
natural antipathy between the Zimbo and the
himbo: or, to give them their full names, Duncan
Fletcher and Andrew Flintoff.

One unfortunate side-effect of the previous series had been Flintoff's
transformation into a super-larrikin. Visibly wasted at the Trafalgar
Square parade, he was becoming almost as well known for stumbling
around behind dark glasses as he was for hitting sixes. His recreational
habits were never going to endear him to Fletcher, whose twin
obsessions were dedicated training and loyalty to the team.

So why, you might well ask, did Fletcher appoint Flintoff
as captain 18 months later? The answer – to borrow Lyndon
Johnson's favourite phrase – was that Fletcher wanted him inside
the management tent pissing out, rather than the other way around.
(Pissing in inappropriate places, incidentally, had become something
of a Flintoff trope. According to legend, his final act during
those 2005 celebrations had been to relieve himself in the Prime
Minister's garden.)

The other obvious candidate for the captaincy was Andrew
Strauss, an NCO-type who was far more up Fletcher's street. But
Strauss was smart enough not to push himself forward for the post.
He realised that Flintoff had transcended cricket to a level not seen
since Botham. Anyone who stood between 'Our Fred' and the top
job would be pilloried, especially by the tabloid papers that saw
him as a latter-day George Best.

It was soon evident that Strauss had made the right decision,
certainly for himself and probably for the long-term future of the
England team. Within a couple of Tests, the 2006–07 tour was

'You, mate, are making me concentrate.'
Warne, en route to 71 from 65 balls at Sydney,
thanks Collingwood for sledging him

careering downhill like a rusty shopping trolley. Meanwhile Flintoff was suffering a relapse of his persistent ankle injury and realising the truth of the old saw 'Be careful what you wish for'. By the one-day series at the end of the Tests, he was self-medicating with ever-increasing volumes of booze.

'You just hope the players do not let you down,' wrote Fletcher in his autobiography, *Behind the Shades*. 'Sadly Flintoff did. We arranged a fielding practice in Sydney. He turned up still under the influence of alcohol. He was in such a state he could not throw properly. He had to pass the ball to the bloke next to him to do so.

'When it came to trying to catch the ball I honestly thought I was going to hurt him, so uncoordinated was he. I was fuming and stopped the practice early. Remember: this was the England captain in this state. I had to calm down and think what to do.'

Flintoff's father would later call this story 'a betrayal', as if invoking the old stag party rule that 'What goes on tour stays on tour.' Fletcher responded that he would have kept quiet, if only Flintoff hadn't gone and got even more publicly trashed during the Caribbean World Cup two months later.

That second flashpoint arrived after England had suffered a dismal six-wicket defeat to New Zealand in their opening match in St Lucia. Flintoff allowed himself to be talked into a restorative drink, and then – in his own words – 'I realised I'd had enough and slipped out. Instead of walking down the road, I decided it would be nicer down the beach . . . A row of kayaks caught my eye, but none of them had any oars.

Next to them were some pedalos, and I remember dragging one to the edge of the water – presumably because I fancied a ride. But for the life of me, I couldn't work out how to get on it – or my legs into it – so I let go of it, and it quickly

**'You can talk,
mate, when you've
achieved something.'**
Ricky Ponting counter-
sledges Paul Nixon

Shane Warne and Chris Read exchange words during the fifth Test at Sydney. Paul Collingwood, whose countersledging of Australia's champion of 'mental disintegration' was largely counterproductive, looks on

drifted away from the shore. I think I slipped and fell over in a few inches of water, but nothing more.'

The next morning, the 'Fredalo' incident – as it soon became known – was reported in the *News Of The World*, and Flintoff found himself suspended for the following match against Canada. It might sound like an innocuous indiscretion, but after the debacle of the Ashes tour, his seaside splash was seen as evidence of a toxic drinking culture within the England team.

The perception was not far wide of reality. Vaughan would later offer the following snapshot of the one-day leg of the Australian odyssey. 'I basically opened up my captain's suite at the hotel as a kind of free bar to the touring party . . . We were like a throwback to the 1970s. And we just about kept it away from Duncan, although I should think he suspected.' Alarmingly, the running joke in the dressing-room was that 'This drinking team has a cricket problem.'

Vaughan's justification was that 'the lads needed some refreshment in all senses'. And he may have been right, at that: England rallied to win their last four one-day games and snatch a late consolation in the form of the Commonwealth Bank Series trophy.

In reality, though, this was what financiers refer to as a 'dead-cat bounce' – a small and short-lived hike in the value of a fast-falling stock. By the time England reached the World Cup, the cat had stopped bouncing, but it was still getting smashed. The Fredalo fallout was widely blamed for England's low morale during the tournament, in which they failed to beat anyone but the minnows in a live match. Dropping his guard for once, Fletcher wept during the

R.T. PONTING (AUS.) 576 runs at 82.28

S.R. CLARK (AUS.) 26 wkts at 17.03

England lost heavily in Brisbane and capitulated horribly in Adelaide. By the time they reached Perth, the *Sunday Telegraph's* long-serving correspondent Scyld Berry reckoned they were 'more crushed and crestfallen than any England team I have seen in 30 years'. There was to be no let-up from a frighteningly focused Australia. The implacable Ponting and the near-undismissible Mike Hussey (458 runs at 91.60) did passable imitations of Bradman; Stuart Clark lost nothing in comparison with the evergreen McGrath (21 wickets at 23.90); and the indomitable Warne (23 wickets at 30.34, plus 196 runs at 49.00) outpointed Flintoff as an all-rounder. Fittingly, McGrath joined Warne in retirement after the Sydney Test. His long-cherished 5–0 whitewash was in the bag at last.

team's final training session as he announced he was stepping down.

There was something heroic about Flintoff's dissipation, and the havoc it wrought on the Fletcher regime. From the nadir of 1999 – when England stood at the bottom of the Test ranking table – the team's fortunes had been revived through a southern African amalgam of discipline and common-sense. Flintoff had played as central a role in that climb as anyone. And yet, when the time came for him and Fletcher to work together as captain and coach, we saw how fundamentally incompatible they were.

'Duncan used to talk about the terrorists within a team,' said assistant coach Matthew Maynard. 'You need them in your side but you know they will cause some problems too, and that you have to bring them into the circle. It's about getting the balance right – the critical mass, as he always said. He wanted eight good characters who could drag the weaker ones through, one who might be a quieter lad and two who were tougher to handle.'

For all his savant-like ability to deconstruct a batting technique, Fletcher had never fully understood his senior seam bowlers – an

It ain't over until the fat boy spins. With a final career tally of 708 Test wickets (195 of them English), the retiring Shane Warne waves to the crowd after Australia's whitewash-clinching victory at Sydney

often truculent bunch who included Matthew Hoggard and Steve
Harmison, Flintoff's closest ally. Now, as England lurched towards
humiliation, these so-called terrorists were threatening to take over
the asylum. There was little need for the Australians to initiate
verbal battles with a clique-ridden team that was slowly tearing
itself apart. Not that that stopped the ever-combative Warne. In
the last of his eight Ashes series, the bumptious blond bowed out
with a verbal tirade against Paul Collingwood in Sydney. 'You're an
embarrassment! How can you get an MBE for scoring just 17 runs?
Maybe you should give it back!'

Wicketkeeper Chris Read was standing between the two men
(Warne was batting and Collingwood fielding at slip to the bowling
of Monty Panesar), yet he remained silent as the verbals pinged to
and fro. It was a revealing moment. During the glory days of 2005,
England had been uniquely united. Now, just 18 months later, they
had slipped back into the bad old days – pre-Fletcher and pre-central
contracts – when the national team was just a loose collection of
individuals.

So it was that Fletcher finished his time as England coach with
a grim record in Australia:
nine defeats in ten Tests.
It was the only blot on an
otherwise excellent record.

Still, he had done
something to pave the
way for his successor. He
had saved Strauss from the
ignominy of leading the most
ill-fated expedition since
Captain Scott. 'You might
thank me for this one day,'
he told Flintoff's second-in-
command, when the squad
was announced in September
2006. By January 2011, the
whole of English cricket
would have reason to agree.

THE DODGY DOSSIER

The rudest comments levelled during the 2009 Ashes stemmed from an Australian who wasn't even in the side any more. After the 2006–07 whitewash, Justin Langer had retired from Test cricket and taken up a post captaining Somerset. Now, in the lead-up to the next Anglo-Australian battle, he prepared what Alistair Campbell might call a 'dodgy dossier' on the strengths and weaknesses – well, weaknesses mainly – of English cricket.

Langer also had a role as Australia's batting coach, and the document was supposedly intended for the squad's eyes only. But someone found a hard copy lying around the dressing-room at Sophia Gardens in Cardiff, where it had been left in the aftermath of the first Test, and passed it on to the former Glamorgan opener Steve James, now a reporter on the *Sunday Telegraph*.

Was this a genuine accident? Or could the Aussies have been looking to inflict a little psychological damage? They did have previous when it came to misplaced documents. In 2001, their professorial coach John Buchanan had slipped a handout filled with mystic quotes from the Chinese warlord Sun Tzu under a series of doors in the team hotel – including one belonging to the Press Association's correspondent.

But while Buchanan's meanderings were largely incomprehensible (Mark Waugh, one of the more hard-headed members of the squad, forwarded

> **'I don't think this Australia side has an aura about them.'**
> **Andrew Strauss tells it like it is**

'Can be a bit of a pussy when he is worn down.' Justin Langer's acerbic remark about James Anderson, the leader of England's attack, could just as well have applied to Mitchell Johnson of Australia

his straight into the wastepaper basket), Langer's offered precise, sometimes personal critiques of the opposition.

English cricketers, he began, 'are great front runners . . . [but] they are the best in the world at tapering off when things go flat for them. This is also a time when most of them make all sorts of excuses and start looking around to point the finger at everyone else – it is a classic English trait from my experience.'

The next paragraph continued 'English players rarely believe in themselves. Aggressive batting, running and body language will soon have them staring at their bootlaces rather than in the eyes of their opponent – it is just how they are built. They like being friendly and "matey" because it makes them feel comfortable. In essence this is maybe the key to the whole English psyche – they like being comfortable.'

It was all good knockabout stuff. And it gained extra credibility because it came from a hard nut like Langer. His own Australian team – the one that ruled the world for at least a decade – had actively relished adversity. Langer's mentor and role model Steve Waugh was so determined to challenge himself that he called his autobiography *Out Of My Comfort Zone*.

Unfortunately, these giants of the game had now repaired to the great commentary box in the sky. And Australia's new recruits were at least as flaky as the opposition. No one stared at his bootlaces with as much intensity that summer as Mitchell Johnson, a left-arm

'Heck, Bill Gordon might even receive an MBE.'

Malcolm Conn, writing in *The Australian*, credits The Oval groundsman with engineering Australia's decisive defeat

seamer who sprayed it around like a leaky fire-hose. It was ironic that Langer's pithy assessment of England's main seamer James Anderson – 'can be a bit of a pussy when he is worn down' – turned out to be a better fit for the leader of his own attack.

Australia played the more efficient cricket overall in 2009, but England subverted the Langer stereotype by turning up when it mattered most. The Lord's Test saw a final flourish from Andrew Flintoff, who had announced his imminent retirement at the start of the match, and followed up with one of his fiercest and finest spells to clinch a 115-run victory. His 'Messiah' celebration pose – in which he dropped to one knee with both arms extended sideways – would become almost as iconic as the 2005 photo he shared with Brett Lee.

Redemption pose: Andrew Flintoff had been to hell and back as captain of the ill-fated 2006–07 Ashes tour, but he bowled superbly at Lord's in his 2009 swansong to turn the Test and the series

The series went to a decider at The Oval, where Flintoff's would-be heir Stuart Broad did the damage in an inspired five-over burst. But most of the chat during that final Test was about the bone-dry pitch. As far as the visiting press were concerned, this was almost on a par with the Fusarium scandal of 1972. *The Australian* newspaper called the playing surface 'dusty . . . dodgy . . . manufactured', while another correspondent said it was the 'first time I've ever seen a drought 22 yards long and three yards wide'. One reporter tried to corner the groundsman, Bill Gordon, who cannily pretended he was called John and offered to pass on a message.

Out of their comfort zone: nobody expected the last-wicket pair of James Anderson and Monty Panesar to survive the final 11.3 overs of the Cardiff Test. But their bloody-minded stand typified England's resolve

The strip was ideal for Graeme Swann, the new England off-spinner who had been turning in some of the best figures since Laker, and who now collected eight wickets in the match. Presumably it would also have been ideal for Swann's opposite number, Nathan Hauritz. But the Australians had committed a catastrophic error of selection, omitting Hauritz in favour of ageing seamer Stuart Clark.

The Aussies' refusal to pick a spinner seemed like a textbook case of shooting yourself in the foot. Yet the pitch recriminations rumbled on, in what seemed a blatant attempt to 'point the finger at everyone else'. Once again, Langer could have been talking about his own team.

2009: 5 TESTS
ENGLAND 2—1

A. J. STRAUSS (ENG.) 474 runs at 52.66

B. W. HILFENHAUS (AUS.) 22 wkts at 27.45

A defiant last-wicket stand in the first Test at Cardiff set up England's bid to regain the Ashes. Tailenders Anderson and Panesar survived for 11.3 overs in that match to claim a draw, and a week later the home team built on their narrow escape by recording a first Ashes victory at Lord's since 1934. Although Australia returned the better statistics overall — they scored eight individual hundreds to England's two — the tourists were undone at key moments by fine English bowling spells. Flintoff was intimidating at Lord's; Broad unplayable when the decisive Oval Test hung in the balance. 'When we were bad we were very bad,' said captain Strauss after the denouement, 'but when we were good we were just good enough.'

THE FINAL FRONTIER

'And gentlemen in England now abed / Shall think themselves accurs'd they were not here'. Andrew Strauss is hardly the type to break into flights of Shakespearian oratory. But as he returned to the dressing room after the opening exchanges of the 2010 Boxing Day Test, even this most unassuming of men must have felt like invoking *Henry V*.

If there is a sporting equivalent of mowing down French cavalrymen at Agincourt, England's cricketers achieved it on that chilly, overcast morning in Melbourne. The visitors were right at home in the murk, and when Strauss won the toss, there was little doubt that he would choose to bowl first. The decision was quickly vindicated as Shane Watson survived two clear chances before gloving a lifter to gully. The bodies of wounded Aussies were soon piling up behind him.

By mid-afternoon, England's seamers already had their feet up in the dressing room, celebrating Australia's meagre total of 98 all out. Then it was Strauss's turn to step into a leading role: he combined with Alistair Cook in an unbroken stand of 157 before the close. With the exception of a couple of dropped catches, his team had approached cricketing perfection. It was a Boxing Day of delights.

For those millions of sleepy fans

'Lovely ground the MCG . . . even when it's half full . . . must have all gone home to watch *Neighbours*.'

Michael Vaughan tweets about the biblical exodus from the stands on Boxing Day afternoon who genuinely were 'in England now abed', the morning ritual of checking the score usually comes tinged with apprehension. Most of us have been beaten into a weary fatalism by the long drought through the 1990s and 2000s. On this great day, though, the hordes of bleary-eyed viewers, listeners and loggers-on could barely believe what they were seeing and hearing. By 8am GMT, as most of them set off for work, the final destination of the 2010–11 Ashes had been settled beyond any reasonable doubt.

'Carlsberg don't do first days at the Test match,' Graeme Swann would later suggest, 'but if they did that was definitely it.' Few Ashes series can have shifted as decisively in three short sessions as this one.

Yet the odd thing was that the two teams had appeared so well matched coming into the MCG. After a drawn opening Test in Brisbane, England had won in Adelaide and lost in Perth. And as 84,000 spectators gathered for the high point of Melbourne's sporting year, the home contingent were confident that the natural

Lord of the dance: Graeme Swann, England's best off-spinner since Jim Laker, was also the team's court jester. His so-called 'Sprinkler Dance' became a running gag throughout the 2010–11 Ashes

order of things – or at least the recent order of things – was about to re-establish itself.

They were about as wrong as it is possible to be. In 2006–07, the final day of the Adelaide Test had represented the point of no return for a haunted England team. In 2010–11, the ugg boot was on the other foot. This nine-hour rout was always going to be the pivotal moment of the series. Australia went on to lose the Melbourne Test by an innings and 157 runs – their heaviest Ashes defeat since Jim Laker's 19-wicket match more than half-a-century earlier. And things didn't improve much in Sydney a week later. This time, they lost by an innings and 83 to complete England's 3–1 series victory.

It was a momentous result. Since Fred 'The Demon' Spofforth

set our narrative wheels in motion, only three England captains have achieved the ultimate accolade: Ashes victories over Australia at home and away. In 2010–11, Strauss joined Mike Brearley and Len Hutton in this most exclusive of cricketing clubs.

Strauss and England had reaped the reward of a precise and rigorous build-up, co-ordinated by another no-nonsense Zimbabwean coach in Andy Flower. Indeed, their planning was so detailed that you wondered if Flower suffered from OCD. Among many innovations, they tested each player to see how much he sweated. Cook was found to be the man with driest hands, so he became the designated ball-polisher and caretaker. And he must have done his job well, because England's seamers were able to find reverse-swing throughout the series, whereas Australia's struggled to move it off the straight.

Cook also turned in 766 runs in the series at a Bradmanesque average of 126.77. This was the fifth-best tally in Ashes history, as well as the second-best by an Englishman after Wally Hammond's 905. And it made a satisfying riposte to the potted biographies in the official series programme, which had been full of catty remarks about the England players.

According to that man-by-man guide, Cook was handicapped by footwork that was 'ever so leaden'. The same programme declared that Ian Bell, who averaged a mere 65.80, 'has been accused of lacking the stomach for a fight'. And that Tim Bresnan, who came in for the final two Tests and performed magnificently with bat and ball, might 'in time be viewed as a jack-of-all-trades makeweight'.

I know what you're thinking. After Langer's dossier had backfired so horribly 18 months earlier, the Aussies had gone and made the same mistake all over again. There was a quirk to the story this time, in that the biographies had actually been commissioned from an English reporter. But still, Cricket Australia were the ones putting the programme together. And the content clearly riled the England team, in a way that translated into a of extra motivation.

'...happy few.' By leading England to Ashes victories

at home and away, Andrew Strauss joined Mike Brearley and

Len Hutton in the most exclusive of cricketing clubs

'Whoever it was who wrote those profiles, he obviously thought England have got no chance,' said Swann after the series. 'He backed the wrong team.'

And so, after 130 years in which the Ashes urn had switched hands 22 times, the same truisms still applied. You can taunt the opposition, you can wind them up, you can even cheat them out of their wickets. But, as W.G. Grace had discovered all the way back at the very beginning, you had better have enough firepower to back up the posturing. Sledging sounds a hell of a lot more convincing when it comes from the winning side.

2010–11: 5 TESTS
ENGLAND 3–1

A. N. COOK (ENG) — 766 runs at 127.66

J. M. ANDERSON (ENG) — 24 wkts at 26.04

As in the previous series, England escaped from a tight corner in the opening Test. They conceded a first-innings lead of 221 at Brisbane, thanks largely to a Siddle hat-trick, but fought back so powerfully that they eventually declared their second innings on an absurd 517 for one (Cook 235 not out). From then on, the tourists were almost totally dominant, with the exception of a riveting afternoon in Perth when fast left-armer Johnson rediscovered his radar and his lethal inswinger. The other three Tests — in Adelaide, Melbourne and Sydney — resulted in innings victories for England, who thus won an Ashes series in Australia for the first time in 24 years.

INDEX OF PLAYERS

Roman page references indicate that the player is mentioned in the narrative text, in a scorebox or in a display quotation; **bold** page references indicate that the player is the principal subject of an entire section; *italic* page references indicate that the player appears in a photograph.

PICTURE ACKNOWLEDGEMENTS

The publishers would like to thank the following agencies and individuals for the right to use their images in this publication:

Getty: 16, 20, 21, 23, 29, 32, 36, 38, 41, 44, 45, 48, 50, 55, 62, 66, 73, 80, 83, 86, 90, 95, 98, 101, 102, 105, 116, 123, 126, 128, 132, 135, 139, 140, 145, 146, 154, 156, 163, 167, 168, 171, 172, 175, 176, 190, 196, 210, 215, 217, 225, 226, 245, 251, 261, 269, 271, 272, 275, 280–1, 283, 284

PA Archive/Press Association: 286, 287, 288, 291, 292, 294

Patrick Eagar: 181, 185, 193, 199, 205, 223, 230, 235, 237, 241, 247, 265

David Frith: 27, 76, 107, 110, 120

Reuters: 284

SW Pix: 254